Lillie Holliday

THE VOICE OF OMAR SHARIFF THORNTON

THE THREAT OF INJUSTICE

LILLIE HOLLIDAY
THE VOICE OF OMAR SHARIFF THORNTON

Author: Lillie Holliday

Contact information: **OST Memorial Foundation** page on Facebook

Lillie Holliday

Email: lillie4holiday@gmail.com

Publishing: ToReign Publishing

References:

Rapper Eminem's "I'm not Afraid" released (2005)

Dr. Martin Luther King, Jr. "Injustice Anywhere is A Threat to Justice Everywhere.", Letter from Birmingham Jail, April 16, 1963

All photos from Lillie Holliday's family collection.

Copyright

All rights reserved. No part of this book may be reproduced or transmitted in any form or by any means without written permission from the author.

ISBN: 13-978-152347977

ISBN: 10-1523479175

Printed in USA

In order to protect the victims, those still grieving from this ordeal, and those who do not wish to be mentioned. Names have been omitted. But this story should be told.

This book is not about me, Lillie Holliday. This story is about my son, Omar Shariff Thornton. His life, his struggles and his side of the story!

INTRODUCTION

As I sit here this New Year's night, January 1st 2016. I am just memorizing my baby and I'm thinking about the fact that I will never see him again.

I'll never be able to hug him again and I will never be able to tell him I love him again.

I will never see any of his kids and he will never be married.

I will never know what kind of wife he may have chosen and I will never know what he could have become because his life was cut so short.

I will never hear his laughter nor will I receive another surprise. No more calls ever again.

My life has definitely changed forever.

May his soul rest in peace and may God have mercy on me for my life is forever shattered and it will definitely never be the same way again.

LILLIE HOLLIDAY
THE VOICE OF OMAR SHARIFF THORNTON

THE VOICE OF OMAR SHARIFF THORNTON

AS WRITTEN BY LILLIE HOLLIDAY

HIS MOM WITH LOVE

(The world was Omar's as he posed for a picture on his first state to state driving job in Texas).

Special Thanks

I would like to thank all of the people who have shown support and encouragement over the years. Your words and inspiration has kept me strong and able to keep Omar's memory alive.

Lilies

LILLIE HOLLIDAY
THE VOICE OF OMAR SHARIFF THORNTON

PREFACE

Tragedy struck me on August 3, 2010, when my son, Omar Shariff Thornton lost his life.

In the pursuant of the American dream, the obstacles of society, sometimes becomes apparent.

But when faced with the obstacle of racism, it is an issue that is apparent but overlooked and sometimes ignored. But no obstacle is greater than the infliction of Institutional racism.

It changes a man, a woman, or child and takes them out of their natural state of good and puts them into survival mode. Especially when survival is challenged.

What happened to my son, Omar, is tragic. The story is tragic.

But the world needs to know that he was a Good Man... Facing a Cruel World.

But for every ending, there had to be a beginning. And as it stands today, I bring forth to the world Omar's side of this tragic story.

I started writing his story on December the 18th 2010, with a lot of pain and with a huge hole in my heart that will never heal. But I have to let the world know the truth about my son's life. The truth that will reveal that his death occurred long before his own heart stopped beating. But at the hands of a system that failed to protect him and many others that came before him. It was a systematic death at first and that is really what happened to my son...

I don't believe that Omar killed himself. I believe that the people of the company he worked for, killed him.

Just imagine being a mother, receiving a phone call at 7 a.m. and your child telling you that he is going to take his own life.

I know he was in a lot of pain at that moment and now I realize what he had been going through, working with those people at the Hartford Distributors.

I believe that it is the greatest hurt that any parent can ever have and even more so if your child makes himself a human sacrifice for what he believed in. And you know that within his heart, he really believed that it would change things for other people.

I also know that it was far too late to even think about trying to stop him that tragic day. But he will be greatly missed and loved always.

I know that many people would like to know what goes on in the mind of a person who would commit such an act. A person may also wonder where did this person come from, how was his upbringing and what state of mind could he have been in?

Was it something that me, his mother did wrong?

Well there have been many tragedies throughout the world in the last few years with stories that ended the way Omar's did. And I have been contemplating the release of his side of the story for many years now.

But I am his mother and I can only speak for my son, Omar Shariff Thornton.

Part One
Omar Shariff Thornton
His Life

Today is December the 18th, 2010, and I am in a lot of pain right now. There is a hole in my heart that will never heal but I have to let the world know the truth about my son's life.

I was 6 months pregnant with my son before his father found out about him. The year was 1976, and Omar Shariff Thornton was born on April 25th of that same year, at Saint Francis Hospital located in Hartford, Ct.

At birth he weighed only 4 pounds, 10 ounces and he stayed in the hospital for a few weeks until he gained more weight, in order for me to finally bring him home. And at that time I lived on Warren Street in Hartford, Connecticut.

From the early onset of Omar's life, he had been involved in some pretty interesting occurrences. Which of course began when he was born prematurely. But not too long after giving birth to him, he was kidnapped!

It was just so frightening for me and my family and also devastating. I just couldn't believe that my new baby boy was missing. It happened six month's out of the hospital, when he was only seven months old. And so, my boyfriend at that time, and who was *Not* Omar's father, endangered his life and decided to kidnap Omar. I remember contacting the local police and with their effort, they were able to find them. Omar was returned to me that same night, thank God for that.

And at the ripe ole' age of 7 years old, he was also hit by a car.

I was on my way home from work and his older sister was looking after him for an hour. And somehow he wandered off onto the street. He had no broken bones but he was just scared and they kept him in the hospital overnight for observation. I was so thankful that he was okay.

When Omar was still a small baby, I had him christened, at his aunt's church. And once he got older, he would go with her to visit there from time to time. But there was a time when his faith got stronger and he wanted to be taught the word of God. And so he began attending her church more often. But that route left him with so many questions. He was curious about what he saw in that church and the members. So he continued to attend, that is until he figured out that the people there seemed as though they were not very true, and that was his interpretation at that time.

LILLIE HOLLIDAY
THE VOICE OF OMAR SHARIFF THORNTON

And I remembered him always asking me why? He always questioned things that did not seem right in his own heart.

But I feel as though Omar found the answers that he was seeking and shortly after that time, he stopped attending church with her. But it wasn't a surprised because Omar always had his own mind and always made his own decisions, starting from a very early age.

I say that because whenever I would try to punish him, he would take that and turn it into something that made him comfortable. For instance, I would put him on a punishment and instead of getting upset and becoming rebellious, he would turn it into a positive situation for himself.

I remember once, I peeped into his room after putting him on "punishment" and he would be singing or reading or perhaps just playing. In other words, he would never let punishment make him sad. He would find a way to be just fine with the situation by doing something constructive.

(Here's Omar at around 4yrs old, dressed to impress)

And as the years rolled by, I wanted Omar to be involved in things that typical teenagers were involved in at a young age.

I tried different things that I thought he might like such as football, basketball and track but the only thing that seemed to really interest him was math and chess.

He played chess at a very early age, around 5 years old and he was really good at it. It was a game that he really enjoyed and as a result, he even beat some of his teachers playing chess. And interestingly enough, he was taught by that same boyfriend that had kidnapped him as a baby.

Omar was just that kind of kid that actually took care of himself. I would often think that he was put on this earth to fulfill an agenda.

He was a different kind of child. And he had a mind of his own, an independent mind with a spirit like none other.

For instance, when he was around 13 years old he never wanted me to spend my own money to buy him expensive clothes. Especially when I bought him brand name things; he would take them back to the store, get a refund and then go to a less expensive store to buy stuff that did not cost so much. He would then bring me back the change.

And then he would say to me, "When I become a man, I will buy myself brand name things." And he would say, "Right now you have three of us to take care of, including yourself. You don't need to buy expensive stuff and thank you for being my mom."

After that line, I got so emotional, reflecting on those early years, I had to stop writing as the tears rolled down my eyes. A mother's broken heart...

But that was who he was and just the way he thought, from an early age. Oh my god I love him so much. He was such a good son.

And Omar was so thoughtful too. He would often save up his allowance to make sure that he got a gift for me on Mother's Day, Christmas and all throughout the year.

LILLIE HOLLIDAY
THE VOICE OF OMAR SHARIFF THORNTON

And when he was around 5 and 6 years old, he would walk with a stick, telling men that tried to talk to me, "Don't say nothing to my mom!", and he would shake that stick at them. It was just the little things from his heart that meant so much. Like when he would surprise me for my birthday.

He would make it so that before I got out of bed he would present me with birthday cards that he made himself and a birthday cake that he had baked.

Or there would be times when my favorite ice cream would be in the freezer or sometimes he would hide things in my home and call me on the phone and say, "Mom there is something in your house that I left for you but you have to find it." And then he would start laughing and say "If you're in the living room you are very close."

He was the type of person that if he could make you smile, that would make him happy. Omar had such a big heart, even as a young child. It's just so much I miss about him. And when I think about what kind of child he was and what kind of man he turned out to be, it made me know all too well that he was put on this earth for different reason

I realized at an early age that Omar's father was never going to be a real father to his own child. That was even evident one day, when I took Omar, as a baby to meet his paternal grandmother. Omar's father had already informed his mother that he was not his child. So she just wanted the both of us to go away.

So I went away. And I did it with frustration and disappointment. But I knew from the beginning that his father was upset because I wanted him to pay child support and because of that situation he had decided to act as if he really didn't care about him. And would only see Omar when he felt like seeing him.

I remember when he came to visit him one day, Omar was 9 years old. He gave him a basketball and my son cherished that basketball because that was the first thing that his father ever gave to him.

But over the years, I stopped Omar from waiting for his father.

I got tired of seeing my son's disappointment when this man would promise to pick him up and would never show up. And he did it so many times that I stopped telling Omar that his father was planning to come and get him. That way, if he showed up, good. But if he didn't show up, Omar would not be hurting, waiting to see his dad.

I just remembered him looking so sad. And it hurts my heart that his father never spent quality time with him.

But a few years went by and one day his father just showed up again. I remember that Omar was about 10 or 11 years old at the time. That day he gave him a ring that he took off of his finger and Omar loved that ring.

That was the second thing that he ever gave to him, and it was the last.

Although I knew the truth about who his father was and his father knew that he was the father because he had taken the blood test when he was a baby, I waited around for almost 12 years for him to give Omar his last name and he refused to do it, so I finally took him to court. The judge stated that he had already taken the blood test and if it comes out again that he is 99.9% the father, "I will change his name to your last name whether you want it or not."

I wanted Omar's last name changed to Thornton, and at that time, Omar's last name was my Ex-husband's last name.

I wanted it changed but his father was still not willing to change it. Although he had taken two paternity tests that determined that he was the father, he was still not willing to accept it.

So finally the judge changed my son's name and his father was so upset because of what the judge said to him. And when we got into the elevator after court, he looked Omar in the eyes and he said, "That's why you don't have no father."

What his father said to him hurt me so bad that I was speechless. And I will never know how that one statement affected Omar. I just hugged my baby and we walked away. I said to him, "You have a mother and that will be enough, I love you."

He never apologized to my son for that... And that was the end of their relationship for what they did have.

But Omar had male figures that he looked up to in his life like his aunt's husband, the same aunt that he attended church with. He liked to have fun with his nephews and would pay for Omar and his brother to attend boxing,

LILLIE HOLLIDAY
THE VOICE OF OMAR SHARIFF THORNTON

wrestling and many other entertainment shows that kids liked to attend. And they had a good relationship.

He was also the uncle that after having a few drinks, liked to chase Omar with a little harmless pocket knife, he was only joking and it was non-threatening. But one day at an early age, Omar had got on the school bus and decided to mimic how his uncle played with him. He chased some of the kids that were on the bus with a pocket knife as if he was going to cut them, all in humor but someone reported it to the principle. And he had the nerve to suggest that Omar needed special education. And when Omar went. Needless to say, he did not like that little yellow bus that they made him ride in.

A few weeks after that happened, Omar and some of his friends were playing outside. One of them threw a rock and a car window ended up broken.

The cops showed up at my door and I asked the police officer to pretend he was going to arrest Omar. That scared him so bad and his eyes were so full of water that he promised that he would not get into any more trouble if the police officer would not take him to jail. He was around seven years old at that time.

He was so active that my landlord use to call him the "devil". But to me he was just doing what little boys do every now and then.

He had a favorite cousin that he was very close to. He was an older cousin but he treated Omar as if he was his little brother and my son looked up to him. And he use to hang out with him.

But a few years later, this particular cousin had gotten arrested for dealing drugs and got put into incarceration. That devastated Omar.

From early on, Omar liked to work. I remember when Omar was around 10 years old, his first job was delivering newspapers and when he turned 11 years old, he got a job working with his uncle, unloading watermelons off trucks. His next job was passing out meals in the park.

When he started that job, we were still living in Hartford. But when I decided to move to Manchester, CT, Omar started saving his money so that he could buy a bike to ride back and forth to work from Manchester to Hartford. And that is what he did for the rest of the summer.

Everything was going well until I enrolled him into Manchester High School and that is when things started to change.

It was almost every other week that they would call me from the school to tell me that Omar would not remove his hat or he didn't take his jacket off or something of that nature.

It was almost as if they were determined not to let him be comfortable while he was there. But I didn't realize how serious it was, being there. Until the end of the school term, when they would not let him graduate from school. It was so serious that he had to go to East Hartford High school in order to graduate and finish high school.

It was as simple as going there, taking the test and getting his diploma.

But before he graduated, Omar was in a work program through the school where the students worked if they wanted to and of course he was very happy to know that he could have a part time job.

Omar was so excited, that he couldn't wait to come home and tell me about the work program at the school. And the next thing I knew he was telling me that he had gotten a job working with Dean Machine Cleaning and doing assembly work. And he worked there part-time during the school season. He liked the job because he was making his own money. Even after graduation, he started working full time. And he actually worked more than 40 hours a week, eventually wanting to become permanently hired so that he could be entitled to some benefits and vacation pay. And despite the fact that they said no, he kept on working there.

But after a while, they had him cleaning the bathrooms and working on the assembly line and driving the van. He was actually doing quite a few jobs but he did not mind working hard. It's just that he wanted to be treated equally.

And when he realized that it was not going to happen, he said to me, "Mom, I do everything they ask of me and they still don't want to treat me fairly. So I am NOT asking them for a full time job anymore. As of tomorrow, I am giving them my two weeks' notice! "And he did.

He also said that he would not accept any offers from that company. And sure enough, when they made the offer to give him a pay raise after he gave the two weeks' notice and a full time job with all the benefits, Omar refused to accept because he wanted to know why they couldn't just accept him in the first place.

LILLIE HOLLIDAY
THE VOICE OF OMAR SHARIFF THORNTON

So he left that company and started working for JC Penney's shipping and receiving. Of course he had a car that he bought himself and that was also very stressful for him because almost every week the police pulled him and his friends over. They would have them get out of the car, search their pockets and find nothing and then let them go.

It was happening so much that I had to go down to the Manchester police station and ask them to leave my son alone.

I asked them to take a look at his car so that they would know not to keep harassing him.

But Omar was not discouraged and while he attended school, Omar and his brother would sell clothes out of the back of their car as a side hustle. That is until one morning he went outside and not only his car but his brother's car was destroyed.

After that happened, he started putting his money together for the next car. He bought the next car from a woman in Manchester but after giving her the money for the car, he found out that the car would not pass inspection.

And of course she did not want to give him his money back, so I had to step in once again and help him get it.

The only reason she decided to give Omar his money back was because of the fact that I took some guy friends over to her house and waited in front of her house every single afternoon.

She would see us sitting there near her house; but it was not until one day when, I guess her husband must have gotten upset and afraid. He finally came over to us and said, "I have nothing to do with what she's doing." We said ok and then I guess at that point he must have told her the same thing. So she decide to give us the money back and we gave her the car.

But it was always like that and as a result Omar did not have very good luck in buying used cars.

Meanwhile, straight out of high school the credit cards were coming from all over the place. And at that time, Omar did not understand the meaning of credit and how it works. So he spent all the money on the credit cards which was about 1,800 dollars. A year later, he started to realize that credit was important and he wanted to restore his credit. So he went to an attorney in Manchester to file for bankruptcy in order to straighten out his credit.

But later on, he found out that the attorney did not help him at all. And he had been misinformed because the attorney charged him $800 to file the bankruptcy. But it made Omar unable to restore his credit for 7 years. And the money he paid the attorney was only just about half of the debt that he owed his creditors. That made him realize that that attorney just wanted to make life hard for him.

And once Omar got it, he said, "I have learned my lesson." But thankfully, he restored his credit eventually and moved on from that ordeal.

While he was working at JC Penney's, Omar decided to go to truck driving school for his class A license and eventually he fulfilled all of the hazmat requirements that goes with the Class A licenses which would enable him to drive tractor trailer trucks.

Shortly after that, he went to college to get a degree in the medical field because he was well aware of the benefits of having options, he said to me, "I need more than just a truck driver's license because the police can take that license whenever they want to." And he was so aggravated by the police officers that he just didn't trust them.

Omar had a lot of different jobs when he was alive. He always believed in having a job and always believed in bettering himself. And he would always find a job that was better than the last one that he held.

He let his job know that he was leaving after he graduated from getting his class A driver's license and started working, delivering appliances.

And during that time, Omar went to his brother's apartment and saw that he was not doing so good financially and offered to pay for him to go to school and get his own CDL license. And eventually his brother got his license. That is when he found a job that they could both work together, traveling from state to state.

Omar paid for his brother's CDL license and his brother never had to pay him back. He also paid for me to go and get my nurse's aide license, I paid him back every single penny even though he didn't want me to but I did anyway. He was just that kind.

LILLIE HOLLIDAY
THE VOICE OF OMAR SHARIFF THORNTON

I remember one day when he saw his nephew walking, he had a hole in the back of his jeans and the only thing that came to Omar's mind was mom. Omar said to me, "I will give you the money to go shopping for him." that's the kind of heart he had.

If only his uncles felt that same way about him, maybe his life would have been different.

I'll never forget the time when we went down south and he asked his uncle to help him get a truck and he said, "I will pay you back the money." and he told him, "No, it's better if you do it on your own."

His uncle would not help him, so Omar took the time to find a job for him and his brother so that they could drive together.

That didn't work out too well because his brother kept on crashing the truck, smoking cigarettes and the police kept pulling them over until finally Omar said no more. And also the company that they drove for, made them pay for the gas themselves and that company had them turn in the gas receipts without reimbursing them so that they could claim it on their tax returns.

But during the time that they worked for the company, Omar wanted to save money, so he would only eat one meal a day.

And as history would repeat, almost every other day, the police pulled them over.

One day the police pulled them over and started acting like they were the suspects that had robbed a donut shop in Chicago earlier that day. Despite the fact that they were operating a 24 foot box truck.

So they had to get out, put their hands behind their backs all while they had guns pointed at them. And of course, they were afraid. That was not the only time the police did that to them. And it was so bad that I became afraid for my sons and I wanted them to stop driving from state to state.

It was just too much for Omar during that time though; for one thing his brother smoked cigarettes and that was irritating him because he did not smoke and it was a lot of other things that was going on with his brother. He just wanted to get off the road and he was not making any money; only the man he was working for made money.

But he still believed that the trucking business was his own business and he was his own boss. In fact the first trucking company that he started was called Carl's & Robert's trucking.

Omar liked that idea so much that when he got back, he decided to contact a trucking company out of Canada and I went to Canada with him.

On our way to Canada, Omar had a gas can filled with gasoline in the back of the car and I said to him "What are you doing with that gasoline?" He would just say "Don't worry about that mom." So I said "Okay."

So as we were getting into Canada, I was tired from driving 8 hours to get there. Omar had fallen asleep and I didn't really pay any attention to the fact that we were really out of the United States.

When I pulled up to the immigration booth, not thinking, as I was also tired. They asked me if I had any guns in the car and I said "no" because I just wanted to keep on going. But they still had me to pull over and they asked me, again "Do you have any weapons in the car?" and that time I said "yes" we do we have two guns in the car.

Boy did I wake up after that!

And then they said "We should put him in jail." and I told them that Omar was asleep and he did not know what was going on. But they decided to search the car and when they found them, they took our guns. And had the nerve to take all the money that we had brought with us, cash and credit cards. And even though we had all of our legal paperwork for the guns, all the while they were still threatening to put Omar in jail.

I actually fell down on my knees and begged them to let him go. I was the one that told them that we had no guns in the car, not him.

So after they took everything we had, including our money. They let us go but we had quite a few miles left before we would reach our destination. Which was where the truck was waiting to be picked up.

But the problem was, no money, no gasoline.

I had no idea what we were going to do because we had a distance to go before we could have gotten to any gas station. And that is when we used the gas that Omar had stored. Strangely enough, it was almost as if he knew something was going to go wrong.

LILLIE HOLLIDAY
THE VOICE OF OMAR SHARIFF THORNTON

We had just enough fuel to get to a place to call my other son for money because we still had to pick up the tractor trailer.

And finally, he picked it up.

On the way back, it started to rain and ice but Omar kept on driving. And he was driving for so long that I wanted him to pull over and get some rest. But Omar was determined to get to his destination.

He was supposed to bring the tractor trailer to this place but when he arrived and tried to get someone to let him inside of the gate, they would not open it up until the next morning. So he and I slept in the car until that time.

When he went back the next morning, I waited in the car for about an hour until he jumped back in and announced, "Let's go!" And by the sad look on his face I could tell that something was wrong.

I didn't know what happened until about 3 hours later, when he decided to tell me.

What happened was, when he went inside, the company that he was supposed to work for was angry for the fact that he parked the truck on the outside of the fence. And then they went on to tell him that he was disqualified as a driver for that company.

My heart hurt so badly because he did not have a job after all and he had lost all of his money and time. He tried so hard and it just didn't work out.

But that did not end there with the trip to Canada. We ended up going to court with them and for about 2 years through mail and at the end they decided to keep the guns and the money, so that was another loss for Omar. That was one of the worst trips he had ever taken in his life and it was almost like Murphy's Law. Everything that could go wrong, went wrong, but he just kept fighting and trying to get where he wanted to go in his life. He never had just one thing to deal with and at times it was almost quite a few things at one time but he would find a way to land on his feet.

I often wonder; if Omar didn't lose his life at such an early age, what would he be doing right now? He was such a brilliant young man. And the most special thing about him was that he loved people and that he always wanted to help others.

And it didn't matter how hard it was, he would always try to help someone out. He was just that good of a person that he would meet someone for the first time and lend a helping hand. He would lend money to a stranger by just taking their word.

Of course some would try to take advantage of his kind, giving heart and of course if I found out about it, I would get involved and get his money back for him. And it happened very often. Which caused him to be called a "mama's boy".

Omar was the kind of man anyone could have depended on. And he never wanted to just exist. He wanted to make a difference, an impact on people.

And he was always there for his family too.

He was always there for his brother and sister even though since Omar passed away his sister doesn't really have anything to do with what I'm doing now but he was there for her. Despite how she treated him when he was alive.

In fact, he actually helped me get a rental car to go down south to get her son while she was incarcerated. And then when she got free and came back to Connecticut, he helped her with some of the things that she needed and he also let her use his laptop. She destroyed it by putting water inside his laptop. When he wanted it back she was just so evil to him.

And he helped me with her son by buying all of his clothing. He did so much more for her and her sons in fact he was the one that was with her when she had her oldest son.

I remember one day when I had my daughter's son and Omar had just received a ring, one of the only gifts from his father. He was a young kid and he was helping his sister with her baby by changing his diaper. He had removed the ring to wash his hands and next thing I knew, my daughter left the house. She had stolen the ring from Omar.

I tried my very best to replace the ring by buying him a similar one.

But that did not dampen his spirit, he just kept on being his giving self.

And I remember how he would help his nephews with money for clothing.

LILLIE HOLLIDAY
THE VOICE OF OMAR SHARIFF THORNTON

The list goes on and on. It was such an often occurrence that when he passed away, I wondered what happened to all of his money. He was a hardworking man, so I know that there had to be some left behind.

But then people started coming to me telling me how much Omar had helped them and changed the course of their lives.

They would tell me things like how he would offer to pay for them to go to school or he would give them money to help get a car, so that they could get to work.

His friends would say that it didn't matter what it was, he just wanted them to do better.

And there was one time when a lady friend of Omar's', told me that she had a house fire and lost everything. It was my son Omar who put them in a hotel and paid for it. And not only that, he also helped them get back on their feet.

Omar was a young man that had no biological kids of his own but he had kids that he helped to take care of. There were also kids that only got things from him and he made sure that they always got what they needed, even though he didn't have to do those things, he did them anyway.

And I had a woman tell me a story about when she was outside trying to clean her windows; how my son pulled over, got out of his car and cleaned them for her.

There were so many stories like those about Omar. And I've had so many people tell me that his niceness never ended. They would tell me that he was just a decent human being. And that they always wondered who his mother was who had raised him to be the way he was.

He had so much respect for everyone, so many people would say to me that he was just an amazing young man and I would say, "Yes he was."

And every time I think about who my son Omar was, and how he touched so many people's lives in his short life, the tears start rolling down my face. And as I reflect on those years, I have to bring myself to stop writing. The pain is too sharp, a part of me is gone forever. May God help me through this because bringing his story to the world and having to think about all of the memories that we built together as a family, has been the hardest thing I've ever had to do.

Omar had a saying that he would say all the time, "I came into this world when I wanted to and I will leave when I'm ready."

A statement that is pretty powerful which I never paid any attention to it until now. But ever since he had been born premature and then released from the hospital a few weeks later and then left this life at 34 years of age, it is something for me to think about.

Omar knew the day that he was going to exit out of this world. He had planned that day out.

And another thing that I thought was strange, was the fact that it didn't matter what he did for someone or how much money they borrowed from him or how much he helped them, he would never ask for anything back. Not even the money they borrowed. Deep down, he knew that he would not be needing those things back.

He always believed in respect and he would always say to me, "Mom, I remember the man that respects me and the one that disrespects me."

Omar believed in bonds and the belief in a man's word, so if he gave you his word, you can bet your life on it that he was going to do whatever it took to do what he said he would do.

That's the kind of man he was. And that is how I want him to be remembered.

Today the world is missing a good person. And it's no telling what he might have been. No telling where he would be in his life if he had not suffered so greatly from the effects of institutional racism and all of its forms.

My heart gets full and heavy every time I talk about my son because I know that they did him wrong. And all that he wanted was to work towards the American dream.

And in his short life, Omar went through so many different changes. At one particular time, I can remember, Omar had some business dealings with these people in New Jersey. And Omar was the kind of person that believed that when you talked to someone and there was an agreement, their word was their bond. And his word was his bond.

LILLIE HOLLIDAY
THE VOICE OF OMAR SHARIFF THORNTON

And if he told you something, or made a commitment. He would do exactly what he said he was going to do.

I remember when he wanted to buy a truck from some place in New Jersey. The people held about $3,000 for longer than 6 months. But Omar never actually received any trucks from that company. Until I found out about it and got his money back.

Shortly after that time, Omar had purchased about three or four trucks from this trucking company out of Windsor, Ct. And the agreement that he had made with this company was that if he brought some buyers in to purchase trucks from them. He would receive a 10% referral fee on each sale.

And brought people to purchase trucks he did.

He had made so many referrals that some of the people that he had sent to this company, paid in cash. But the trucking company defaulted on their agreement and they never gave him the 10% referral fee that they had promised him. And that was a serious problem. In fact they were always trying to find ways to make money off of him. For instance, they were selling him trucks that weren't in the best condition. And at one point, they had him paying for the repairs of a truck while paying for a truck that he was renting so that he could keep working. And he was so stressed out that I went over to his house one day and he was laying on the floor.

I could tell something was really wrong and then he started telling me how he was trying to pay for a rental truck to keep working. He also told me about how he was paying for the repairs that the company was doing on the truck. A truck that he had bought from them, I was so upset about what he was going through. The warranty should have still been on the truck but those people were so greedy that they just tried to take everything from him. But me being a mom, I decided to take matters into my own hands. Enough was enough.

So one day I got dressed up and I went over to that company and I had a conversation with them. I told them that what they were doing was wrong and I needed them to rewrite another contract. And I also needed them to take responsibility for the repairs and pay for the rental that Omar had gotten from them.

I guess they did not know who I was but it didn't matter because they knew that they were wrong.

I even went so far as to bring a contract with me. And yes they signed it, relieving Omar of the responsibility of paying for the truck that they knew they should have been paying for. They even gave him back the money for the rental and paid for the repairs.

Omar was so happy how everything turned out and he just told his friends that he had a really good lawyer.

Just imagine having a big company with so much money and yet they would have the nerve to take all that they could take from someone like Omar.

Although he had to deal with unscrupulous behavior, that didn't stop my son. And at that point, he owned three or four trucks that he had bought from that trucking company.

He started his own trucking company because he wanted to put his own trucks on the road. That's exactly what he did, so he started working for a company that needed him to deliver mattresses and they had a lot of work for him.

At that time the diesel was almost $5 a gallon and he was still okay with it. Until the gas prices went down and then all of a sudden the company didn't have any work for his trucks.

It was quite apparent that they used Omar and his trucks when prices on diesel was very high, making it hard to make any money off of the work that he did.

And also once the price of diesel fuel went down, the company started bringing back their favorite trucking contractors to work with.

That stressed him out a little bit but he was ok. He never gave up or threw in the towel, he just thought that he would go elsewhere and maybe things would be different.

So one day, Omar had gotten some information from a company that he had business dealings with about a company that he could work for.

LILLIE HOLLIDAY
THE VOICE OF OMAR SHARIFF THORNTON

After they recommended him, he went to the company, filled out the application and immediately started working for them.

And that was the start of Omar making deliveries from Connecticut to the borders of New York. He worked himself so hard that he knew that he would be getting a very good paycheck.

At least he should have been getting a good paycheck, right? Wrong.

Once again, the evils of the greedy world reared its' ugly head and at the end of two weeks his paycheck was dismal. That company had only paid him $350, which was not even enough to put diesel fuel in his truck for the week.

Needless to say that Omar was disappointed when he picked up that check. He couldn't believe it. And that was enough for him, so he decided not to work for that company any longer.

And then I noticed that after Omar had passed away, that same company tried to make it appear as though they had paid him $1,600 per week and that's definitely not true. It was truly strange how things had been happening to him.

But not too long after leaving that contract, Omar started working for a company that delivered hair products. He said he loved everything about that job and he worked there for some time. Sadly and not so long after working for that company, he found out that they were going out of business.

He couldn't believe it. Here it was, a place where he finally liked and they were going out of business. It just didn't add up.

And that weekend he was driving in a suburban area and the police pulled him over in his car and gave him a speeding ticket for going 5 miles over the speed limit. And due to the fact that he had hired an attorney for representation for whatever state he would be in, he thought that he would be just fine anyway.

But he made the error of telling the police officer that he had a class A license and that a speeding ticket would be bad on it for his job.

The police officer wrote the ticket anyway and he had to go to court. It was there that the judge set the highest penalties for him and told him that he would have to pay a fine, and to make matters worse, they suspended his license.

They were using him as an example and I didn't realize it then but I realize it now. Omar was always fighting against all odds.

He just kept getting one bad break after another.

For example, one day someone broke into his apartment and took a lot of stuff and did some damage.

Omar had two different apartment insurances and neither one of them paid him. He had done what he was supposed to by calling the police after he got home. He was so frustrated that he did not make a claim to one of them.

The police came out and made the report that his apartment was broken into and vandalized but when he applied to the insurance company the only thing that they could come up with is that they were not going to pay him. They did not honor the agreement.

His laptop was taken and when he let them know that, they said okay we will buy you another laptop. But he said no, "I don't want you to buy me a laptop. I want you to do what you're supposed to do."

His window was broken and it was unsafe due to the fact that he lived close to the train tracks. And they were supposed to give him the opportunity to stay in a hotel where he could feel safe. They did not offer those options to him. The only thing that they did was humiliate him in every way and aggravate him.

That is when they started having meetings with him. They wanted him to drive up to Orange, Connecticut once a week to have meetings with them. And in the end, they never gave him anything that they were supposed to.

Finally he just said that he couldn't take it anymore. No more time off of work and he just let it go.

It was just one more, sad thing that happened to him and on top of that, they never refunded him back any of the money he paid them monthly.

It was sad because for all the time that he paid them, they just took his money and never gave him anything even in the time of need as agreed.

LILLIE HOLLIDAY
THE VOICE OF OMAR SHARIFF THORNTON

He was just a young black man, in the midst of a corrupted system that society deemed as being ok.

Omar was so young and he was trying so hard. And trying to do the right things. But of course, that was not enough.

I will never forget one Black Friday, when he called me up at 3:30 a.m. in the morning.

"Let's go down to the store." he said to me, "We're going to get that flat screen today." And I said ok.

It was Omar, his girlfriend and I who had gone down to the store were we stood in line and waited so long, that he had to go across the street to get us some breakfast from McDonalds, although we were probably the 4th or the fifth person's in line.

And finally the doors opened up and we went straight to the televisions.

And by the time we got to them, it was one white man standing there with six TVs. This man also had 5 other people in the store to help him purchase them because you were only supposed to get one.

So I went to get one of them and the white man said "No, this is mine.", so then Omar went to get one and the same man said, "No that's mine too."

Omar walked away looking so sad and I even felt bad because he had his heart and mind set on getting that TV for me. And that was the only thing that we wanted. So when we were about to leave, the man tapped Omar on his shoulder and said, "Young man you can have this one."

And Omar was thankful for that.

I believe that the man thought about it and looked at how humble Omar was, being such a big guy. And I think that it touched the man's heart, how he just let things go rather than argue or try to get them to do the right thing.

I would get angry at him sometimes for being so kind hearted when he should be protesting.

Like one time when I went to turned the key in, for the apartment that he moved out of.

He had the key to the doors for 3 days after he moved, and of course he gave notice that he was moving. But when I turned in the keys for him, the property manager says, "I'm keeping the security deposit because he had the keys for 3 days." She had the nerve to tell me that, even though the apartment was empty.

I couldn't believe it but Omar did not want to argue about it and allowed her to keep his money. I couldn't do anything about it and he told me to just let it go.

And there were times that he would bring home his friends and ask me to let them stay with us because they had nowhere to go.

And there was one friend in particular, who Omar asked me to let stay with us. He had the nerve to get up and start making breakfast for himself, that next morning, as if that was his house.

Omar got a little upset about that, but then said to him, "Ok, you can stay but you have to stay in the basement." And that's where his friend stayed for a while.

And then he had this other friend that he would take back and forth to work. That particular friend was living with his father and stepmother and he was having a rough time, so Omar made himself obligated to start dropping him off and picking him up from work, even though he himself had to get to work.

But he still did it because that guy was one of his best friends. They played basketball together, they talked to girls together, and they just did a lot of things together. And then one day, his friend's father decided to send him down south to live, for whatever reason.

And the next thing that we knew, his best friend got shot and was found dead. And that was very painful for Omar. His best friend's father brought pictures to Omar's classroom and Omar was very upset at the fact that he would show him pictures of his best friend, dead.

Omar said, "Why would he bring those kind of pictures to me with my best friend laying in the casket?"

LILLIE HOLLIDAY
THE VOICE OF OMAR SHARIFF THORNTON

That was a really bad day for him and it seemed as though things kept happening to him on a regular basis.

I always said that Omar had learned too much, too soon because he would see how different life was for white people. He always had quite a few white friends and they would hang out together. They would go into stores together and the people would follow him and his other black friends around while the white kids stole candy. As a matter of fact, his white friends stole a whole lot of things and was NEVER watched or noticed. That is an example of how Omar learned about being black and the difference in the way his white friends were treated. Their actions were either ignored or simply overlooked due to the color of their skin while the black kids were being watched.

It is now that I just didn't realize how much he was learning at a very early age, and so he got to realize the different ways that he was being treated. He noticed those things and those things, he knew, deep down, was not right. . A fact that would surface later on in life.

And it was from that early age that he started dealing with that treatment, in his own way.

But little did I know, it all had taken effect on him and I did not know what he was going through. I was blinded by the fact that he would be alright because I instilled in him, the value of being equal to everyone.

Omar was exposed to so many things that it hurt me then and it hurts when I talk about it. And that thing, that big thing was Racism.

It makes a person cringe just to think about what Omar was up against. And to make matters worse, my son really didn't have any family support. That would include no support from his uncles, aunts, cousins or his father. Sadly, I was majorly the only support that he had at that time.

Omar would always stand by his family members but they never stood by him. And for Omar, that was another major thing in his life because he would always trust people and he would always help them, especially his family.

But when he needed them, they would not be there for him. That kind of family treatment was something that I had hoped that Omar would never have to go through. It was just simply too much for a person to deal with.

He gave way too much and got back way too little. But that's just the way it was, even with his friends. And at some point they started behaving more like users.

They used him so bad, even to the point where it seemed like they had no respect for him.

And yes, I am going to be his voice and say it because Omar is not here to defend himself. And I am not going to name any names. But one example of a total disrespect by one of his so called friends, was that he couldn't wait for my son to pass away, so that he could get involved with an ex- girlfriend of Omar's.

So that speaks to what kind of friends he had and how they really felt about him.

Maybe he had a couple that we're really good friends, that I know of. But I think that's because Omar freely helped people, they just thought that he was someone at some point, that didn't matter to them.

And was the same kind of thing like with family. He would be there for his friends but if he needed them, they would not be there for him.

He went through that a lot. It even got to the point where I could see that he was stressed out from dealing with some of his friends.

Or how one of his best friends supposedly helped him one time in his life when he needed him. But it came to light that this person was not really a true friend.

Especially when something that Omar could never have imagined happened to him at the hands of that friend.

That particular person tried to start a fight with Omar on the very job that he hired him for. And it took Omar some time before he could bring himself to tell me about that. It was just a lot of hurtful things that my son had to endure. Things that I was unaware that was happening and that was one of them.

I think that things happened to him in such a way sometimes because he just wanted to do the right thing and treat people right.

LILLIE HOLLIDAY
THE VOICE OF OMAR SHARIFF THORNTON

He was so strong and never stopped trying to make sure that he got things right when he was determined. And he made sure that he was not going to have babies all over town, by different women.

Omar always said to me that if he was going to be a father, he wanted to build a foundation first; he wanted to have something to offer any child of his own.

I know that his upbringing had something to do with his value system and his thoughts on becoming a father could have also come from me because when he was around 11 years old, I had that conversation with him about babies and women.

I made sure that he knew not to ever leave it up to the woman to be the sole provider for a child, it would be just as much of his own responsibility. And I let him know that he needed to protect himself as well. So I gave him condoms and I told him that was *Not* permission to have sex but if he was going to do so, he needed to understand the responsibilities of it all.

And to my understanding, he ended a few of his relationships, due to the fact that they wanted a baby and he was not ready for that kind of commitment.

Omar was at the point where he just wanted to move on with his life, while his brother and sister did the total opposite and just didn't care about life like he did.

But that was not a surprise because Omar was just different. And he had so many different things to deal with.

In all the years that I have had the pleasure of having him in my life, I had never seen Omar break down and cry. And I don't know, maybe it was because he never saw me break down and cry.

But if he can see me now, he's seeing many tears fall far too many times, running down my face.

But there were fun memories, good memories of Omar before his passing. He was just a fun loving kind of guy, in cruel, cruel world.

Omar and his brother were big guys but they would rather run then to fight. And at some point, I said he was kind of scary.

I remember one day when I came home. Both Omar and his brother's wallet and keys were on the table. I thought something was unusual about that and worried that something might have happened to them. They even left the juice that they were drinking; the glasses were still sitting there on the table. But their shoes were still there.

So I'm thinking, "What happened... did they just disappear?"

What happened was, they had dashed upstairs to my room, both of them holding the door shut.

I asked, "What's going on?" and they said, "Mom there is a bat out there flying around!"

I laughed. Now here it was, these two big ole' grown men hiding in my bedroom, from a bat! They said "Yes we're scared and we're not coming out."

I opened up the door and ran them out of my room. Sure enough the bat had already flew out because they scared it by just running.

And it was more funny stuff like that happening over the years.

And I remember a funny story when Omar and his brother drove to Texas. Omar called me at like 2:30 in the morning and said "Mom, Edward is chasing me around the truck. Tell him to stop."

I started laughing and then I can hear him laughing. I said, "If y'all don't stop, the police is going to shoot both of you, thinking that you are robbing somebody." They were just fooling around like brothers do and those were the kind of fun loving situations that occurred when Omar was alive and I remember talking to them for a while before going back to bed that night.

But that's how life was with me and them. They were my boys and both of them would always call me whenever something was wrong. And I loved how they would call me when things were right as well.

LILLIE HOLLIDAY
THE VOICE OF OMAR SHARIFF THORNTON

Omar! Tears are starting to roll down my face because he never kept anything from me and that's why I said that he kept a secret from me and he never did that before.

I never forget the time when Omar said, "I am taking you out to eat."

And I said, "Okay but I want to eat at Ruby Tuesday's."

Omar said, "Okay let's go."

After we finished eating, he started laughing and called his brother.

And said, "She did not have enough to eat. Now I wonder if she wants to go to McDonalds." and he started laughing and his brother started laughing. I was the big joke for those two.

Yes my sons were "Momma's Boys" because we were very close and whenever you saw me you saw my sons.

Everyone that knows me, knew how close I was to them. And they knew how close they are to me. We were like each other's keepers and there was nothing that could come between us.

We hung out together the majority of the time. Even the photograph that the media keep's showing of my son on every August 3rd. The day that Omar lost his life, is a picture from when we were together.

We were in New Haven shopping at the flea market about 15 years ago. In that particular picture, Omar looked hardcore and rough which the media chose to portray him as being because they want him to appear to be a monster but he was no monster.

He was just a good man, gone too soon. And he was someone suffering from post-traumatic stress disorder caused by "institutional racism" at his place of employment.

My baby, god knows I miss him. And I always will.

But it must have taken a lot out of him to really be pushed over the edge. To be willing to give up his life because he loved himself some mom and he always wanted to protect me.

So I know that they had to do a lot of stuff to him towards the end in order to give him that frame of mind. For him to want to die!

I'm crying again. I have to stop now and I can't do anymore.

I am hurting so bad and I pray to God. No mother should ever have to go through what I'm going through.

Even when Omar was a baby he was a good baby, never really cried a lot. And for most of the time you would not know he was in the house. So it's so hard to understand how he could be driven to the edge and how that type of situation could elevate so strongly.

But there is always a reason for everything and I don't know why God gave this job to me. I don't know why my baby was chosen to end his life that way and I don't have all of the answers.

But I just know that everything happens for a reason and that's just what I know.

When he was growing up, my attention was mainly on his sister and brother. And after his devilish age, somewhere between birth and around eight years old, Omar started seeing life differently. I mean by the way he started doing things in his own way.

Omar started to save whatever money he made and he didn't want fancy stuff. He developed a mind of his own and at a very early age. He had what I would call a strong determination despite the fact that he always had a lot of obstacles in his way. But he kept going over, under and around them to make things happen.

Omar was a no-nonsense type of person and he spent the majority of his life being very serious. It was like he was always on a mission. And there were certain things he had to accomplish. It just seemed like there was never enough time.

He would just sit still and have a clear mind. And he was always thinking about how he could get to a better place in his life and how he could help other people get to a better place.

And here I am, once again. God knows that I love that little boy and the tears cannot stop rolling down my face.

There is a hole in my heart that will never heal.

LILLIE HOLLIDAY
THE VOICE OF OMAR SHARIFF THORNTON

Omar and I having good times

In Omar's whole life I never heard him use bad language because he had so much respect for me and for people. I never heard his brother use bad language either.

I remember when I had foot surgery and I had to sit in one of those chairs to get around in the grocery store, one of those little car chairs that you drive around in the store. Omar was with me and he was making all kinds of jokes but he was right there with me. Actually this is at the time that he was working at the Hartford Distributors and when he wanted to take time off to help take care of me, they threatened to fire him if he took time off. But he decided that family was more important and he did not fear getting fired. He took three days off to be with me, despite the threat.

That was a funny time, and he had me laughing.

Omar always had those little funny ways about him.

You could be sad and when he came around, he would find a way to make you laugh. And that would be the highlight of the day.

He just loved making people happy.

I can't help but wonder if Omar was still alive, what would he be doing right now?

I always think of how much better he could have made his life and how he loved going to school to learn taking different types of trades.

Or how he could have better prepared himself to meet this world on its terms.

Truth be told, the Hartford Distributors company was only one part of what happened to Omar.

Near the end of his life, he was dying long before that day.

I wish they could have just treated him like a man. That would have made the difference between life and death, and I believe that he would still be alive today. And those 8 other people that died, would still be alive.

I think that everyone should always respect each other and I think life will be better for everyone.

And for Omar it was always about respect.

Omar would always say to me, "I will always respect the man that respects me and I will never forget the man that respects me. And I will never forget the one that disrespects me."

I never forget when Omar had a dentist appointment at this black dentist office and Omar paid that dentist $2,500 off of his credit card to do some dental work for him and after going there a couple of times one of the guys that was cleaning Omar's teeth said "You know I smoke reefer?" and that was enough for Omar. He did not want to go back to that office again and the dentist kept the $2,500 without finishing the work; and this was a black dentist. That's just the way things were done at that particular office. He had so many disappointments throughout his life, but he didn't give up, he just kept on fighting even though it was just so overwhelming.

Omar had dealt with so much in his life and Hartford Distributors was the straw that broke the camel's back. If I can use that term a little.

Did they know that they had pushed an extraordinary person over the edge?

And that is just a sad time in America and I wish I could turn back the hands of time.

LILLIE HOLLIDAY
THE VOICE OF OMAR SHARIFF THORNTON

But the harassment started early on for Omar, so much that he said to me, every time a police officer stopped him, they would try to find something that they could charge him for (A prophecy that would one day be fulfilled).

But anyways, one day, the police had Omar and his girlfriend sitting out on the corner for about 2 hours while they waited for a police officer to bring a book to find out if the knife that he possessed was of legal length. And this was all over a knife that was within the guidelines of what it should have been and he also had a new 9 millimeter Glock in the glove compartment of the car. But because he did have a gun permit, they wanted to find a way to take it away from him. But that did not work, so they just kept going at him and as a mother I never expected that they would treat my son that way. Especially because of the color of his skin. And this occurred almost every other week.

The police officers would pull him over and try to find anything that they could get him convicted for or perhaps arrest him for something, so that they can take away his gun permit.

They would give him a ticket for something petty and would never let him go. And when he would plead "not guilty", the judge would give him the highest penalty. And that is when he started to lose faith in the "Justice" system.

That is why when he talked to the police during the 911 call, he said to them, "You guys are going to kill me." He just did not trust them at all.

But not giving up, he decided to go to New Jersey and put money down on a truck for himself. But that particular company kept his money for about 3 months until I found out about it and called them. Omar was so tired of trying to get his money back from them, that he just gave up.

But I made them send the money to me overnight after telling them that he was in the process of getting a truck from a different company and he needed that money back. And that is how I did it.

Omar finally bought a truck. And he was very happy because it felt good to become his own boss.

So then he started delivering mattresses and bed frames. Things were going good, as he was helping his girlfriend with her bills. He also decided to move into his own apartment.

Not to say that they broke up or parted ways. They were still friends in fact they were still together, just not living together.

And when he found an apartment he had to give them a deposit of $2,500, even though he had very good credit and the rent was only $625 a month. He knew that wasn't right but he accepted it and moved in.

Shortly after that, Omar decided that he wanted to buy more trucks and put them on with this company delivering beds.

He put on three trucks with that company and started working with them when diesel fuel was almost $5 a gallon. And then as soon as the diesel fuel went down to $2, the company told him that they no longer needed him because of the recession, work was slow.

That was very stressful for him because he now had four men out of work, including himself and three trucks to make payments on.

With no jobs to work on, as a self-contractor a person has no rights. You cannot collect unemployment and you have no benefits. And when they tell you that they don't need you anymore, they have the right to hold your last checks for about 6 weeks. So you are really on your own and it takes time to try to get another company to take your truck on.

So he decided to find another company to put his trucks on and in the meantime make his payments on the trucks.

It wasn't easy because those companies took so much money from the contractors.

The guys that actually did the hard work, could hardly make it financially. But Omar still tried to make a living out of it despite the fact that he could barely afford to pay for the repairs. And in Omar's case he hired all people that he knew, like friends and family. And that didn't make matters better because they thought he had more money than he really had.

At one point he started picking up things off the street to sell, trying to keep things together.

LILLIE HOLLIDAY
THE VOICE OF OMAR SHARIFF THORNTON

But he started paying them too much money, something like $800 a week. It was just too much and he bought GPS's for all the trucks.

He just thought that if he did everything he could to help them, they would be good employees but that did not happen.

He would tell me, many times what was really going on and how his best friends wanted to fight him on the job. That hurt him so bad because that was the first time he really needed his best friend. That just took a lot out of him because he was always there for his friend and never needed him before that day. They didn't have respect for him and now they thought he had so much more because he was willing to give up so much to them.

Little did they know, he only had a big heart.

And as time went by, I could see the hurt and pain.

But when I was around him, I loved him so much and as a mother it was one of the greatest pains to watch your child fall and you cannot pick him up.

But Omar was always on the move and he would be constantly looking for new opportunities. Like one day, he saw a job in the paper and said to me "This job is paying good money but I don't know where it is."
He would say that a job was just business, you keep looking for better and that's what he would do.

So he responded to the job advertisement and told me that they wanted to meet him at a hotel to fill out an application.

Of course, I did not want him to do that because he would be meeting total strangers and giving up too much of his person information. Especially to someone that he doesn't know anything about.

But he said to me, "Mom, I don't have anything left to lose!"

Hearing him say that gave me the chills and I just didn't know what to do. I cried that night and I prayed to God that things would get better for him. But today, now I know that my son was walking into the Devil's Den...

He finally did find a job working for a company out of Boston. And after working with them for a while he got a call from the place where he had previously put in the application at that hotel.

The new company wanted to meet with him and he was very excited about it.

And when he went to meet with them, he found out it was the "Hartford Distributors". They needed a driver for their beer deliveries. He also found out that they had a union, which he thought would give him some job security.

So when The Hartford Distributors Company asked Omar to come work with them, he gave his other job a two weeks' notice. And he started working for his new job from 11 p.m. till 7 a.m. which made it possible for him to work both jobs until he finished the last two weeks of the old job.

He wanted to give them consideration, allowing the Boston company time to replace him and he also did not want to go a week without pay. Especially since he had people that worked for him, which he had to pay.

So when the Boston company overnighted his paycheck, they suddenly decided to cancel the check once they realized that he really was going to quit working for them. And, despite the fact that he even gave them ample notice.

He did not discover that the check was cancelled until he attempted to take out money from his bank account to pay the people that worked for him. His account came up negative and he did not understand why. Upset, Omar went down to the bank and that's when they informed him that the company cancelled the check.

Again this was very upsetting and it would be for anyone because at that time, the cost of diesel fuel was almost $5 a gallon.

He had already paid for the gas and he also had employees that were waiting for their paychecks!

But being the kind of man he was, he didn't want his employees to be without their payment, so he paid them out of the Hartford Distributors paycheck.

Omar was angry! But I told him not to worry, he could take them to court and the judge will make them give him back the money. So he followed my advice and filed a claim against them. And after a few weeks, it was time for the court date

I went to court with him that day. And of course the representative of the Boston company was there too. But it seemed like every time Omar tried to speak, the judge would tell him to be quiet. She told him that she had heard enough from him but let the man from Boston stand there telling a bunch of lies!

They started telling the judge that Omar was driving the truck all around Hartford, all times of night. And that they had to send men from Boston to find the truck and at the same time they told the judge he had $40,000 worth of items on it.

She never asked them why they didn't call the police or if they had a police report. She just believed whatever they said without presenting any evidence. Omar lost the case.

But if she would have only listened to Omar, she would have known that they were lying because Omar was working two jobs, one from 11 p.m. to 7 a.m. and the other job from 7:30 a.m. to 6:30 p.m.

So he didn't have much time to ride around the city with a truck no less get any sleep. So there was no way he could have done that, but the judge just looked at him and acted like she just didn't care.

I don't know if it was because he was a young black man; maybe we will never know but I never thought I would see the day when a judge would take sides with a company. Helping them take money from an honestly earned paycheck from a hardworking man. A man that worked hard to make his deliveries and a man responsible for paying his employees, as well as having to cover his own expenses.

And when the judge made the decision to allow that company to take hard earned money from a poor young man, doing the right thing. It hurt my heart. But what she did not realize is that her decision was almost like a person throwing a live grenade into a burning fire.

That was an injustice, a breakdown of the system in my opinion. And this is just another episode of "Institutional Racism" for my son, Omar Shariff Thornton.

And to make matters worse; while this was going on, his paycheck was being garnished by the IRS. It was all due to the fact that he had been paying his employees $800 a week without taking out taxes. The IRS took out everything except $120 a week.

I don't know what Omar was thinking and the guys that worked for him thought that my son had a lot of money but in all actuality, he was paying them more than he could afford to.

It had gotten to the point where he was out picking up scrap metal off the street to sell. I just can't imagine all of the things that my son was dealing with in those days.

Like before he lost his court case Omar had traded in his truck and bought a new car. And then the engine went in it, so he was also dealing with that. And before that took place he had to pay $2,500 to move into his apartment.

But he started the job working for the Hartford Distributers, nevertheless and from day one, things just didn't seem right.

Part Two
Omar Shariff Thornton
The Hartford Distributors

I remember Omar being very excited about working for the Hartford Distributers. He thought that everything was going to be alright because they were supposed to have a great Union and he just knew that his rights would be protected, finally. He thought that the union would fight for his rights and he was very happy about that.

And then ironically, things started happening to him and as a result he would complain to the union stewardess and nothing would change. So he said to me, "Mom, I paid this union and they are not doing anything for me. In fact, they are like a family playing a game, working together to take away the rights of the people of color." he said, "I am the only black driver and they do everything they can to not respect me as a man. When I applied to this job, I applied to be a driver. I have 14 years of experience and a class A driver's license. I have traveled from state to state, doing deliveries and they still decided to put me in the warehouse to work for a year and a half but I wanted to be a driver. I want to drive so badly for that company, so I worked in the warehouse and I did whatever they asked of me."

From what I understand and I am not sure how true it was, the few black employees who did work there worked in the warehouse "basement" as packers.

And after working in the warehouse for so many months, one day they decided to ask Omar to go and make deliveries in a truck. This was his first time going out in their truck and it was the biggest snow storm ever yet still he said ok.

"They gave me a full tractor-trailer to deliver by myself and I did it. And they were surprised and then I went back to work at the warehouse the next day. It was almost like they just wanted to see if I would have crashed the truck in the snow storm. Then they would have not allowed me to become a driver but I didn't crash the truck, so that didn't seem to make them happy but that made them upset. And then when I did finally become a driver, they started changing the rules. But I figured I would be able to deal with it because I wanted a good job."

So Omar tried to deal with almost anything that they threw at him, just so he could have a good job that had a union that would make them treat him as a human being, but that didn't happen.

LILLIE HOLLIDAY
THE VOICE OF OMAR SHARIFF THORNTON

The Union stewardess and the company, they were made up of a family that worked in cahoots with each other that maintained the culture of racism and discrimination, maybe to uphold the status quo. They just took his money and worked against him, so he really felt caged in and there was no one else to go to get help. And from what those people were doing to him, it was just too much for him.

He would tell me all of this and I tried to understand. And he would even bring home papers where he had filed complaints but they never did anything about it.

I remember when he came home one day with a cut on his leg. He said that a male co-worker had did it with a forklift and he complained about it and nothing was done. He said that the next day when he returned to work, the man just laughed at him. That job had to be very stressful for him.

And Omar would tell me that the majority of the drivers that he worked with at the Hartford Distributers would not so much as say hello to him or talk to him, only if they *had* to say something. And they would not respond to him if he spoke to them, it was just a hostile situation.

Omar had a cellphone that was connected to a headset that resembled a walkie-talkie radio set and little did they know it was actually a phone. And they were ok with that.

It would be many mornings that I would be talking to him while he was wearing his headset and 80% of the time I would get upset when I would hear him say to them, "Don't talk to me like that. I am a man, show me some respect!"

It was bad enough for him with all of the issues going on with his personal life, but now he was working in an environment where the staff tried everything they could to aggravate him. And for no reason at all they would be petty about every little thing. They would complain about anything that they could complain about and they would write him up for it.

He said to me in frustration one day, "It doesn't matter how hard I work, they still just want to aggravate me." he said, "I am the only black driver and it seems like they hate me."

And then they decided to change all the rules when he became a driver. It was very common that whenever you did not deliver a load of beer and you brought back some of it, you would still get paid for it. But once Omar became a driver, they told him that he could not bring back anything, and that everything had to be delivered.

And as a driver, things got no better. He was just so stressed out as the mistreatment continued.

He told me about a time when he had left a cup in the truck and was written up for it. Or when he and a young co-worker worked together doing deliveries. And while out on the "run", that man hit a car and totaled it. He was convinced that he was going to lose his job. But then the police officer came and gave the man a warning. And all that he got when he got back to the job was four days off and because he was never written him up, they had to pay him for the four days that they made him take off. When you're on the outside looking in, this all does not add up.

And Omar knew that if it would have been him, he would not have a job because it was just a couple of months before that happened; the police stopped him for going 2 miles over the speed limit in his car. They gave him a ticket that he had to go to court for and the judge would not throw it out. Even though he had no prior bad driving record.

So that was another episode of Omar's distrust of the justice system. And he believed that there would never be any justice for him as a black man.

I believe he started to feel like he was caged in. Caged in a world where there was no way out, except for the route that he decided to take that tragic day at The Hartford Distributers.

Institutional racism came at a high cost. Not only at the expense of Omar Thornton's life but it cost many others their lives on that day as well.

But I blame myself in many ways. The system was not set up for him to succeed; it was set up for him to fail in every way. I blame myself for always teaching him, that all men are equal and if you work hard for what you want, everything will be fine.

Omar believed in what I taught him, but that is not what life showed him.

LILLIE HOLLIDAY
THE VOICE OF OMAR SHARIFF THORNTON

And as a hard working mother of three, there is no other way to teach your child but what you know is right and just. But racism is not right and just.

Omar hid a lot of pain inside, and at the end of the day, it was hard for him to except the things that was put in front of him.

I had no idea of all the pain my son was going through at the time and judging by some of the things that he did, I should have realized what was going on.

I should have been paying attention to the fact that he gave so many of his things to his brother. I still didn't figure it out. Or when he took many of his guns and traded them in, I should have known he was up to something but I could never have imagined it would be what he planned.

Oh my god, as I sit here still grieving I would have done anything not to lose my baby. I love him so much and it's just so hard to imagine this world without him.

But there is one thing that I do know, the company Hartford Distributors had an environment of so much hate and racism that it made him angry enough to do whatever it took to stop that behavior. And also because he had done everything he could do to try and get them to respect him as a man.

It was demonstrated though his work ethic and how he would work long hours to make sure that he brought the trucks back empty and did whatever they asked of him. And when he realized that his efforts were not enough, I believe he really got angry then. It changed him for the worse and he just didn't care anymore. Omar was simply tired. But now I know that he did a lot to keep working for that company.

When Omar was a driver for the Hartford Distributors, it was common practice for purchasers to make payments in cash or checks. When he would finished his run, the company headquarters were closed for the day; so drivers were supposed to leave the money in the designated drop box.

And instead of taking it to the company, he would bring thousands of dollars over to where I lived every night before going home. And he would put the money in my downstairs closets. In the morning, before he went to work he would come over and I would throw the money off the porch in a grocery bag because he was afraid to leave the money in the overnight box.

At the time, I was unaware of the fact that the company had a drop box to put money in. I just assumed that they did not have one and he wanted the money to be put in a safe place until he returned to work.

They treated him so badly that he was afraid that they would take the money and blame him for it.

Omar lived in Enfield, CT at the time and he would come all the way to my East Hartford, CT home and pick up the money; and then he would go to work every day in Manchester, CT. And I know that he was one of the best workers that they had because whenever someone didn't show up for work, they would always call Omar and ask him to come in on his day off. And on one of his jobs that they had called him in on, he told me that he did such a good job, that the next morning when he went back to work they were all standing in the hall clapping their hands and telling him what a good job he had done. But then after that, they all went back to their same old, usual behavior.

And in between the bad treatment, they would continue to let him know that he was doing an excellent job. He would do a very outstanding job, according to them, which was a total contradiction to how they treated him.

And Omar knew he was doing everything to the best of his ability and he would make sure that he delivered everything that was on his trucks. Despite the fact that they tried to make him feel like less of a person, I knew that he was more than capable of handling any job that they gave to him. In fact, that job was very easy for him because he was accustomed to traveling from state to state and working with refrigerators/freezers, furniture, washing machines and all types of appliances which was a much harder job to accomplish. And he had done so for about 14 years before he got there. So working for the Hartford Distributors was probably the easiest jobs that he had ever done.

So, anyone could see that he loved working and making a life for himself. And that is all he really wanted. They saw those things but chose to ignore them; they saw how hard he worked, but they just didn't want to tell the truth about what was really going on.

LILLIE HOLLIDAY
THE VOICE OF OMAR SHARIFF THORNTON

And it is a well-known fact around certain communities, through experiences that many people such as Omar and even myself has had, that Manchester, CT is a racist town. I knew that ever since I lived there.

I just never thought my son would have lost his life in Manchester, CT as a result of that cultural "disease", mostly demonstrated to him at the hands of the union and the employees of the Hartford Distributors.

I blame the Hartford Distributors for what happened. That company is at fault for the loss of my son's life; that company is at fault for the loss of the lives of the people he killed. And if they would have just done what was right, just had the right policies in place and discouraged instead of encouraged a culture of racism towards my son, who was a minority, that day would have never happened.

And anyone who knew Omar would tell you that my son was not a violent man.

But when he started working for that company, his life changed so much.

How can everyone that he worked with be so perfect and it be such a tight knit family (company) but yet my son is gone and 8 other people?

But the real story needed to come out and the truth be told. And there would be no more speculation and people would stop wondering what happened.

I am a mother and I know that my son was not perfect but I also know that he was a good person and man that believed in doing the right thing.

As I write this story on behalf of my son, Omar, I think about how close we were and as the memories pour out of me so do the tears. But I can't help but think about the secret that he had kept from me. The one and only secret that he ever kept from me.

Even when it came to the pictures on the cell phone, that's right; I never saw them and I know why.

It was because he knew I would have not allowed him to return to that job. And in his mind, he thought that if he worked to the best of his ability, everything would be ok.

Omar would tell me how easy the work itself was because he was so used to lifting appliances and removing old refrigerators. That was a lot harder than the job he had been doing at the Hartford Distributors. And he had so much experience in that field and he loved that kind of work.

He had made that choice for himself about fourteen years earlier, so I find it so hard to believe that the company would put a private detective behind the only black driver employed with them and have him follow around. And for the amount of beer that they said he took, it was a miscellaneous amount. So I don't know if what they were saying was fabricated or not, because he said the pictures that they showed him at the table before he began shooting, was not of him.

So I am wondering who was truly stealing the beer, that this company was supposedly missing and that would make them follow my son around and why they hadn't investigated other employees who were all white, about pilfering beer as well? And also where is the proof? It is all hearsay to me. At that moment it probably all came back to him so clearly. When Omar told them that the picture that they showed him was not of him, it may have brought him back to the time when he was a child being watched in the stores while his white friends stole candy without being under surveillance.

Yes there was a lot of things that went wrong in that company and racism definitely ran rampant because they came out and said that my son never filed complaints. Which I know was a lie because I saw the paperwork and I know the truth because that was just another covered it up, as usually. I have talked to other people that went through changes with that company, people of color who bore witness to the conditions that my son went through, but I think that they are just too afraid to stand up and tell the truth about how they were treated.

Omar was not afraid and that is one thing that I know in my heart, that he would not stand aside and let that company take advantage of him. So when they tell me that he did not complain to the Union steward, I know that was untrue.

If I know him, I know that Omar did everything in his power to get help.

Respect and principles. That was his discipline...

And I can remember running into one of Omar's friends and he told me how much he respected and loved Omar.

LILLIE HOLLIDAY
THE VOICE OF OMAR SHARIFF THORNTON

He also mentioned the fact that Omar gave him a car. And I was surprised and I didn't know that he had done that. But I always knew that Omar had a very big heart and he believed in helping others.

That's why it is so hard for me to accept what happened to him. I can't sit down and be quiet and stay hush about it. I have to stand up for what's right and make people aware that it is more sides to his story. And what happened was the effect.

But he is definitely a person that is gone too soon. And my life will never be the same.

But I am very grateful for the time I had with him.

When my son was alive, he had such good work ethic. I remember that for him it never mattered how many hours he worked on a job, he would always find time to go to the gym to work out. He believed in taking care of his body and he never smoked or really drank. But he was around 27 years old when he had his first beer and he really didn't like it. So whenever the holidays came around, I would always get sparkling apple cider, so that we could bring in the New Year with a toast.

Just knowing him and knowing what he really stood for, a person would have been amazed. I know when he worked for that company, they were surprised. I could hear them talking to him in ways that they should not have. I know they were looking for him to start yelling and acting inappropriately but that did not happen because he had already been through a lot and he knew how to handle himself. He was not out to disrespect anyone. But it seemed as though the harder he worked the more they would try to disrespect him.

He made an effort to get them to understand that he was a man with feelings and deserved respect. No apologies but this is how I feel. I don't care how much they said that the company was close knit and how they were all one big happy family. I just find that very hard to believe because my son worked there, while being verbally and mentally abused. Now 9 people are dead. Killed in the most tragic way. And all they could say is that, everyone was happy and close.

A person does not go into things, like Omar did and just say, "I'm happy here. These folks are my family." And then decide to commit mass murder.

So something went terribly wrong at that place and those people that worked there need to tell the truth and thank God that they are still alive.

There was one man that said he didn't know why Omar did not kill him. The question is, why did he feel as though he should have been chosen? My theory is that, maybe he was sparred because Omar was hoping that the man would tell the truth about what happen at that company but to me it seems like it was just more lies and more cover ups.

I know my son and I know that he would not have gone to that company with the idea of taking his life and 8 other people's. So I am just wondering will they ever stand up and tell the truth or will this be just like Rodney King's CNN video and they still chose to lie on Martin Luther King Jr., Malcolm X, Nelson Mandela, Hurricané, Emmet Till or Christopher Dorner of California; all of those, who were victims of institutional racism, lies, injustice and cover-ups. Just like Omar but in a different way.

And as a mother, it's not easy but I'm doing my best to try and make the world understand, that he had been through so much. He had been through too much to be only 34 years old. And it had been times when I thought that he would have given up but he didn't. He just kept on fighting with all the odds coming up against him. But it didn't matter how hard he tried, there was always someone there trying to take something away from him.

I tried to be there for him mentally and financially as much as I could and within my power. I tried to support him in every way possible to help him be strong but things just was not good.

But he just could not handle the racism and bigotry that stood in his path, it was just too much for him.

The Hartford Distributors just added fuel and created a fire storm within him and he was not ready for what they were ready to do to him. So when he got there, he was not afraid of hard work. That was a part of him.

But once the acts of strong racism began to take place, everything took on a different phase for him.

LILLIE HOLLIDAY
THE VOICE OF OMAR SHARIFF THORNTON

There were so many things that happened to him there. Sometimes I wonder how he found the strength to keep going on.

I had never seen him angry or very upset, Omar was always calm. And oftentimes he was thinking of ways to put things back together again.

I guess that is why that day when he made his "decision", he was listening to a CD by Eminem "I'm Not Afraid."

I had to really listen to that CD to understand some of what he was feeling inside and connecting his life with what he had been through.

And then it all made sense because every time he went through changes with them. It was always major to him. It was like him against the world. So every time they would do something to him, mentally, it was like a major setback.

I felt his pain and I knew what was going on because I had worked on so many different situations and made people give him back money that they were holding or tried to take from him. At that point, Omar was fighting for survival in this world; fighting for his life.

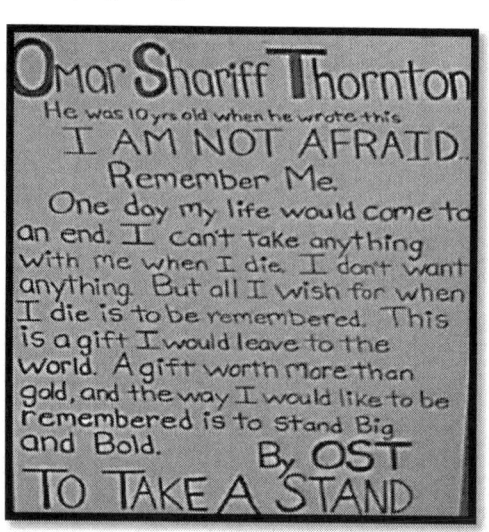

> **Omar Shariff Thornton**
> He was 10 yrs old when he wrote this
> **I AM NOT AFRAID.**
> Remember Me.
> One day my life would come to an end. I can't take anything with me when I die. I don't want anything. But all I wish for when I die is to be remembered. This is a gift I would leave to the world. A gift worth more than gold, and the way I would like to be remembered is to Stand Big and Bold. By OST
> **TO TAKE A STAND**

(Omar wrote this poem at the age of 10 in 1986. Eminem's "I'm Not Afraid." Was released April 29, 2010. An eerie coincidence.)

But he wanted to believe in people and wanted the same type of integrity that he had. And it seemed as though every business situation that he had been in, there was supposed to be that integrity. But at the end of his life he had realized the contrary, he said to me, "I realize now that I really can't trust anyone. Those people just don't tell the truth and they have no intentions of doing the right thing."

He had so much taken away from him, mentally and physically, from dealing with harassment from police officers who would find a way to give him a ticket, or jobs that cheated him out of his money or companies that promised to give him a percentage of money and they didn't do it, to traveling from state to state, delivering items for a company, paying for his own gas. And how they had him keep the gas receipts to make it appears as if they had paid for the gas. And in the end, the Hartford Distributors. It all just added up for him. And it was a toxic cocktail of emotional distress. So in regards to the accusations of Omar stealing beer from The Hartford Distributors, he may have taken beer, I don't know. Anything is possible with the mindset of so much stress that was put on him. It is possible but I cannot say for sure. He was pushed over the edge. But the fact that he may have been taking beer is not the issue, the point is that Omar did not commit murder just because he was being "accused" of stealing a very small amount of product. Let's just set the record straight.

As far as the beer that was allegedly being stolen, Omar was never a thief but he was a man out for revenge when felt he was greatly disrespected. And if he did steal the beer like he was being accused of; I believe in his mind, if he did take anything from that company it wasn't about stealing, it was about taking back his respect.

I know because he had lost all respect for that company and for some of the employees that worked there.

He had even found that there were racist comments written on the walls of the bathroom where he worked. And I would say to him, "Why don't you just leave that job?" and his response would be, "I am NOT starting my life over again!"

And after he said that, I didn't think about it; I figured he was going to do what he would normally do. And that was to work very hard and then after a while they would realize that he just wanted to work and keep his job. Eventually they would start to like him once they really understood him and

LILLIE HOLLIDAY
THE VOICE OF OMAR SHARIFF THORNTON

would drop the harassment once they saw that he would not scream and curse as they expected him to. And that they would see that he was not just some black man with no character.

But the point was that none of them knew how much Omar had already been through before he got to that company.

But Hartford Distributors had to know that he had been going through some things and that he was stressed out because they were withholding most of his pay out of his checks. After Omar paid back taxes owed to the IRS, he was left with only $120 a week.

So during that period of time in his life, my other son and I had to help Omar with money.

They knew that it was a small amount of money that he was receiving from them and they also knew that he was doing all the overtime that he could possibly get so that he could pay the taxes off.

What happened was, Omar's company went down due to the fact that his employees which were friends and family did not have respect for the trucks, the equipment or the job. And as a result, all of his trucks, around three or four broke down at the same time, one cold morning. And he was out of a job. He didn't have any money and that company brought him to court and he missed the court date. Of course the judge awarded the company more money a week then he could afford to pay so he had to get the case reopened again and at that time the judge awarded the company $20 a week. Omar said that after paying them for a while, "I am NOT going to pay them this week. I am going to start sending them $100 a month." But the first week they did not get the $20, they took all the money out of his savings account and he just couldn't believe that he did business with them so long and never missed any payments on anything. This was the same trucking company out of Windsor, Ct that had defaulted on their promise to pay him 10% for every referral purchase to their company. He just couldn't believe that they did that. They made things hard all the way down to the end. He had so much money going out, until he just didn't have the money to pay taxes, plus they have what you call the middle man that controls the contractors which makes it very hard for a subcontractor. The middle man takes most of the money and self-contractors just make do with what they have left.

Omar was surprised when he found out how much money was going to the middleman. He takes from the contractors and then he found out that as black men none of the stores would give them a contract. They give the contracts to white men who turn around and subcontract out to the black men that own the trucks. By the time the white man takes the money for doing nothing, the black man can barely make ends meet.

Omar said it was just a gimmick to get people to work hard so that they could constantly make money off of them for doing nothing. He said that they didn't give you workers comp, they don't give you unemployment and they don't give you medical benefits. And they don't give you enough money to cover those responsibilities. He said that they gave him $400 a day for each truck and each truck had two men working that had to get paid and you still have to pay for gas and repairs and they can fire you whenever they want to. You can have 5 trucks on today and tomorrow they can tell you not to come back and keep your paycheck for six weeks after telling you not to come back. He said it was the worst business anyone could ever be in as a broke man trying to get on your feet. And he also said there was never enough money for you to get medical insurance for yourself or your employees and some means of them to collect unemployment because they never gave you enough money. And as a subcontractor you would hope and pray every day that you didn't have to pay for a repair because that would wipe out the money that they would give you for the entire week or so.

It was hard for him one time when one of the trucks that he bought, he borrowed $10,000 from the bank and gave it to the company that he bought the trucks from. Six weeks later the truck started smoking. When he had it checked it out, he found out that the truck needed a new engine and then right around the same time, he had bought an almost new car and 3 months later the engine was no good in that car, so he had to have a rebuilt engine put in. He paid for that car and then the car was taken away from him after the repairs were done because he could not keep up with the payments. And it was taken from the repair shop.

It was just more money that he had lost.

But then a man tried to take $2,500 that Omar had paid down on an SUV but then later changed his mind about it. And the only reason they gave Omar back his money was due to a mistake they made by sending him the title and in his name. After all that they put him through, he never thought for one second to keep their SUV even though he owned the title. All that he wanted was for them to return his down payment for the SUV. But if it wasn't for the error that they made they would have tried to keep his $2,500.

The bad things just kept happening and I tried to be there for him as much as I could mentally and financially. And as much as I could within my power I tried to support him in every way to keep him strong.

I remember when he was working at the Hartford Distributors and he would tell me how employees of that company would also treat the other black people there. "Its bad mom. They would follow me around or give me the hardest jobs to do."

And there was a black man whose son worked there; he said that when his son hurt his back, they made sure they got rid of him. I believe and know he is telling the truth.

I have even talked to some of the people of color that worked for the Hartford Distributors and they tell me how bad it was there for them as well.

But these same people, even until today, are still afraid to stand up and speak out. To tell the truth about what was happening at the company while they were working there. And to my understanding there is one black man who was a driver that retired from that company, I would love to meet him and hear exactly what he has to say.

But I don't know sometimes, I wonder about our people.

Even at the time when all of these things happened, he always had great respect for relationships that he had with people. Whatever woman he dealt with, if something wasn't right and they couldn't work things out, he would just go on his way. And if they shared an apartment together, he would just let them have everything. He would never take anything that he bought for a girlfriend.

Omar was quite a gentleman and a good man and I am very proud to have been his mother for 34 years. I don't think anyone could have asked for a better son.

One day he was talking to me and he said mom "Do you realize that society isn't concerned about men of color?"
Society is not so much concerned with the guys that already have violations on their record, they are concerned about the ones that don't have any

violations on their records. Those are the ones that they really want to get. And when they pull you over and you have nothing on your record. In Omar's experience with them, the police officer's would get very angry and try as hard as they could to get something on him.

I remember one day, Omar and his friends were crossing the street in downtown Hartford, CT and an undercover police officer bumped into them and said, "What are you going to do about it?" in an aggressive manner and they just kept on walking and then the police officer showed them his badge.

That was a scary moment for him.

Or how one day, he and his brother were together in a car and a white man ran into them, but the police came and said it was no one's fault. My sons could not believe that the police officer would allow that man to get away with running the stop sign and hitting their car. Institutional racism rears its ugly head. Need I say more?

He would always say that the way they talked to him and the things that they did to him, they should have not been allowed to become police officers. But Omar knew that he couldn't do anything about it because at the end of the day, it would be his word against theirs.

And also, Omar felt like he never won anyways, so it didn't matter how much they harassed him. He wouldn't fight back. And after going to court and losing so many times, knowing that he was in the "right"; it starts to make you lose faith in the justice system.

Just like when he was in the process of buying a three family house in New Britain, Ct. The sellers and legal teams, even on Omar's behalf were trying to cheat him and they were all against him. They were trying to get him to buy a house that was faulty and unfit. The sellers thought that he had already signed the paperwork but their lawyer was late and Omar did not sign it and they put the keys on the table for us. That is when Omar and I decided to look at the house fully before the deal was done. And that is when we noticed the hole's in the ceiling and the basement full of water. They thought that they would be able to cheat him on the deal. They still tried to sell him the house anyways but he refused to sign the papers, so they refused to refund him his deposit money. So again Omar went back to court for justice.

LILLIE HOLLIDAY
THE VOICE OF OMAR SHARIFF THORNTON

But he was so nervous and knew that the case would not be judged fairly, he accepted half of the money without seeing a judge. When I asked him why he did that, he stated that there was no justice in the system for him.

And that is exactly what happened to him, he lost faith in the system. He simply didn't believe in it anymore. And that is one of the reasons that prompted him to take matters into his own hands. And he didn't try to get an attorney to help him deal with that company because for most of his life, I have been telling him to believe in the system, take them to court and the truth will come out. But that never happened and that is why things turned out the way they did.

That is a very sad thing in America. To be young and black, and your voice not being heard.

If one time, Omar had gone to court and he had won his case for something that he knew he was in the right; he would have had faith in the justice system. And would not have felt like he needed to take matters into his own hands. I am saying this because I know how much I tried to teach him to believe in doing the right thing and believing in the system that he would have a fair chance.

Now I want to tell you a little bit about the other side of his life. Omar was a very intelligent person and he believed in working hard, respecting other people and he loved his family and friends. And he never had any children. His favorite dessert was banana pudding and chocolate cake.

And whenever he called me from work to cook something for him, most of the time it would be fish and banana pudding.

I miss those calls so much and I'm also going to miss how on his days off, he would say "Mom lets go out to eat or let's go down to the shooting range." We loved shooting at the range.

I miss my baby so much because he was the kind of son that I believe every mother would have thanked God for. And he was always a gentleman. He was never disrespectful and he was very quiet most of the time that you would not know he was in the room unless you said something to him. Those quiet ways reminded me of how much he was like his father. Yes he had some ways like his father but his father did not know that until after he was gone. So many times, I say to myself that he looked just like his father and some ways he was like him too, but they never got to know each other.

But Omar was the type of person that would always try to workout at least 3 times a week and beside that, he loved writing. In fact, he wrote his first poem book at 12 years old!

He was also a very good chess player and Omar enjoyed many activities that kept him busy when he wasn't working, like playing basketball and shooting guns, those were some of his hobbies.

I remember that he liked cooking too. Usually I made his birthday cake but when he was only 14 years old, I was very impressed by the fact that he made my birthday cake and he did a very good job.

I ask God to give me strength to keep on going and it will never be anything that will hurt me more than losing my child.

And when I am alone sometimes, I think about the funny things he would do. For instance he would hide something in my home and call on the phone to tell me to find it and it was for me. It would just be all kinds of different things that he would do. He was just a gentle, kind and loving person. And he always thought about his mom. I love him more than life itself and so many people are coming out telling me how my son change their lives and paid for their schooling. That is what he was really about. Trying to make everyone's life better. If he could, he would give his last dollar and if he thought that someone could get educated and change their life, it didn't matter what color or race they were, he would help. He just had a good heart and was not rich, just a hardworking man who wanted to live and help others. Nothing will hurt me more than losing my child.

I love him so much and he will be forever greatly missed.

I talked about how he didn't want children until he got married but actually he was like a father to many children. He would always make sure that they got things for Christmas and clothes to wear to school. He was just a good person and he worked hard for his money. Yet he still did not mind sharing with others. Omar was put here on this planet for a reason and every day I understand it a little bit better.

He also did some writing, he wrote a few poems that I would like for everyone to have a chance to read. And Omar touched bases with a lot of different things and also mastered a few things as well. He was always smart and was always trying to figure out how to better himself and at the same time be able to help other people. It is very sad that he is not here anymore and I miss him so much that my heart will never stop hurting. This pain will be here for the rest of my life.

But as I said before, Omar liked so many things that it's almost too many to list, the many interests that he had.

But the point that I am trying to make is that, Omar touched so many people in very positive ways.

It has been a month since I stopped writing and now I think I'm ready to continue on.

I have to explain a situation that Omar had with one of his girlfriends. Omar was such a gentleman, especially when he had a situation with a girlfriend of his, at the time. She claimed that she was pregnant with twins. Omar knew that she was lying but decided to give her the benefit of the doubt anyways. But he told me that it was not possible that this girl was pregnant, no less with twins. And of course, not too long after her "good news". She announced that she had lost the twins due to the fact that she had been in a car accident, her mother was very sick and that her brother had passed away in the hospital. Tragic.

But we knew that she couldn't tell the truth about anything and that she had faked a pregnancy. And she was one of the three woman of color that he had dated. The first girl, her family relocated out of the States. The second one, they just grew apart and he was still very young.

His focus was always on building his own life and having something for the future. He was goal oriented even at a very young age and he was always more serious about trying to stabilize his own life. Omar's goal was to be in a comfortable place whenever he was ready to settle down.

I think that he was always serious about relationships because he was very afraid of leaving a child behind like his father did him.

I always taught Omar that all men were equal and that is where I went wrong because his experiences with life were very conflicting. And within himself he knew he was not being treated equal and he noticed that he had to work harder than the white people that he worked with in order to be accepted.

On some of his other jobs, he had experienced a lot of racism just because he was a young black man. I believe at that point he had already given up on trying to have the life that he thought possible. Especially after seeing all the obstacles of racism that he had to face almost every day of his life through police officers and the Manchester, Ct school systems.

And when he first started working from state to state, he would call me and tell me that almost everywhere they went, the police had pulled them over. They even had the nerve to point guns at them one night. He called me and said that the police walked up to the 24 foot truck that they had been sleeping in and woke them up with guns drawn. They wanted to know if they had been to a coffee and donut shop hours before. They had become a part of a robbery investigation!

I was so afraid for their lives that when they decided to stop working from state to state, I was happy.

But at that point, the man he was working for had them pay for the gas that they used in the truck and had them give him the receipts. At the time, Omar didn't know any better because the man wanted to use the receipts as if he had paid for the gas himself, not Omar.

The man was white and they were black and he wanted to give them as less money as he could. They suffered a lot from people that had no justice in their hearts and it is sad just to think that my baby is no longer alive due to racism. It hurts my heart when I think about it.

Racism is the reason why I am in America and because America wanted slaves from Africa, I am African American. Right now it is about 5 a.m. in the morning and I can't get Omar out of my head.

But it just leaves me to wonder how anyone could be so racist towards Omar, he was always so quiet and so easy to get along. He was always willing to do more than his fair share and without asking any questions. All that he wanted was to be treated like a man.

I just can't believe that the color of his skin and racism is the reason why he is no longer here.

LILLIE HOLLIDAY
THE VOICE OF OMAR SHARIFF THORNTON

And as his mother, I love him and I miss him so much. I know that I express that fact a lot but, it's true. And our relationship was the best. He had a way about him that he would find ways to make you laugh, even if you were crying. But he had so many good qualities and I will never be the same.

And now I sit here and I talk about his life but this is supposed to be my son talking about me after I'm gone. But deep in my heart, I know that it is not supposed to be this way. And as his mother, I could see in his eyes when he needed help from me. But even when that occurred, Omar was the type that never wanted me to give him anything. He would always say, "I am a man; I will take care of you."

Yes Omar was quite a son, a very good brother, uncle and a very good friend. He would take care of his nephews as if they were his children and he was very good at it. I can remember when his cousin was incarcerated and Omar was under a lot of pressure but he still found a way to accept those prison calls and send money to him. I can say a lot more about what really happened with him and his cousin.

When his cousin had the opportunity to help Omar out, he passed on returning the favor.

Omar was a person that would help anyone he could and he would never ask you to give him back anything. He would wait for you to come to him and if you never said anything about it, he was okay with that. So many times I had to get his money back from people and companies. He was easy going and they were always trying to take advantage. I had to get companies to redo contracts because they didn't do what they were supposed to do in the contract.

He was never in any trouble. He was always working and he paid for all of his own things.

When he was growing up, most of my attention was to his sister and brother and after his devilish age, somewhere between birth and around eight years old Omar started seeing life differently. I mean by the way he started doing things in his own way.

It was like he started to save whatever money he made and he didn't want fancy stuff. He developed a mind of his own at a very early age and he had what I would call a strong determination.

He has always had a lot of obstacles in his way but he kept going over, under and around them. Almost like he was on some kind of mission. And he was always very smart.

He learned how to play chess at the age of 5 years old and his step dad who gave him his name, Omar Shariff, taught him how to play chess. Sometimes he would play with his teachers at school and he would actually beat that teacher.

He would also play with his cousin and his uncle Wilbert. Those were his two favorite things, chess and math and he also enjoyed playing basketball.

He loved watching it on TV as well. He also enjoyed writing poems and I have about thirty two poems that he wrote when he was around 10 years old.

When he was coming up, I always worked, so every other weekend we would go to the movies, bowling or out to dinner at a buffet or at fancy restaurant and I would always take the kids out to different places so that they could interact with different experiences. I was that type of mother that liked to try and show them different things.

And I can remember like yesterday, when he was growing up. I remember the day when we used to have family meetings once a week at the table for like an hour and everyone would express whatever they were feeling.

We would talk about what needed to be changed or what happened that they didn't like during that week. But Omar was always kind of quiet, never had too much to say and I tried very hard to give him a normal life.

But don't get me wrong, I still say he was not perfect but he had so many good qualities that everyone could appreciate in an individual.

We really had a good time as a family and I mostly raised them by myself with hardly any help. So I had to go extra just to make sure that everyone was okay.

And Omar was always the type that was easy going and it was almost like he was waiting for the time that he can finally take care of himself. He appreciated everything that I did as a mother but Omar just thought it was a lot for me to handle and he couldn't wait to grow up and become a man to take care of himself. He wanted to show me how much he loved me for taking care of him and he was always grateful as a child. He was so appreciative, more than anyone could ever imagine. And he always loved trying to help other people. He always thought as he did, that it would be good for everyone and that was from a very early age.

He was just in a hurry to grow up and he wanted to help me. He also wanted to achieve the American dream.

He was quite a child and he never really wanted anything special.
He was a generous person even to the sacrifice of his own livelihood but Omar was on a mission; trying to do everything that he could to achieve the American dream.

But that's when he realized that the harder he tried, the bigger the elephant got in the room. But he had also experienced institutional racism on his first real job after high school and that was in Manchester. And unfortunately at the time it had always been in Manchester, CT and all throughout his life with their racist ways. It was there in that place and the way Omar was treated while being a black man, sealed his fate at the end of his life. And the more I talk about his life, the more I understand why he said to me, "I am NOT building my life all over again."

I think a part of what happened to Omar was his relationships with white women and white men. He observed how things would happened with them and how the system treated them so differently. It was white privilege, the unspoken rule that made things so easy for them to get away with and how the things that they did would get overlooked.

So he had gotten to a point where he started to get his white friends to buy things for him in order to get them cheaper. So at some point in his life Omar began to understand racism. He didn't have a name for it nor did he really understand racism at first but he just knew that he was being treated differently.

But earlier on in his life, racism never crossed his mind. That is until he began experiencing it firsthand. I did not know these things until later on. I just didn't realize the intensity of his experiences as a black man. He didn't discuss those things with me while he was growing up.

I guess he wanted to figure it all out himself and he was probably more surprised as the days went by because he had many white friends who totally understood how the system was stacked against him.

That is probably the reason why he felt so cornered, at the end of his life. He definitely understood exactly how the white world worked and he knew it was against him. He just decided that he didn't want to handle it anymore. But he wanted to leave a message to the world, that it is time for a change.

And I figured out why some of his last words to me was, "I wish I could have gotten more." Not just at the Hartford Distributors company but the other racist people that hurt him in the past.

That is a very sad thing in 2010 that America should be in a different place. That should had never happened and I certainly hope it doesn't happen again.

He also said to me, "Mom don't be fooled because there is a black president. White people are more racist now than they were before."

When he said that to me, I didn't know that it was probably around the time when he found the noose hanging around the president's neck in the bathroom at the Hartford Distributors.

Even then, they did not try to get help for him.

I said this before, Omar was dying long before 8- 3- 2010. And here is why I believe that August 3rd was the final day for him.

That is the day that was going to be the end of his life and the eight people that pushed him over the edge.

He started planning for that day long before he got there and I believe nothing was going to change that day from happening because he was hurting inside. Hurting from his treatment and hurting from racism. And long before that day, Omar had enough.

He didn't want to hurt anymore and he didn't want them to hurt anyone else anymore.

Before that tragic morning at the Hartford Distributors, Omar packed up almost all of his clothing, gave them to his brother and certain other things that he liked. He stopped cashing his paychecks and he put his jewelry in a secret place. He got rid of the guns that belong to him except for the ones that he was going to use that day.

It doesn't matter what they say about firing him for stealing, his mind was already made up. That day was going to happen and it was nothing they could have done to change it, except treat him like a man.

From the time that he started working for that company that is the only thing, I believe could have changed things.

It was a quite a few things that Omar did before that day, some of them are very personal and I cannot discuss it. I know him, once he got to that point nothing was going to turn him around.

He kept that secret from me and I would have been the only one that could have changed his mind but it was the only secret he kept from me.

One day Omar, his brother and I decided to go to IHop for breakfast and we had a great time! We took pictures that day and Omar was so calm. You would have never guessed that he was going to end his life the next day. Only he knew about it and that was our last breakfast on a Sunday. In that picture, his hair was cut short but every time they show a picture of him, it's with braids in his hair. The picture that when we went to the flea market about 15 years prior. They use that one because they want to make him look like a bad person. And I believe that it's just one more racist act against him. Even in death.

A picture of Omar taken 15 years earlier depicted by the News.

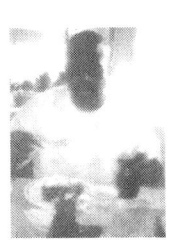

This is the image of Omar the day before he lost his life.

And the people at Hartford Distributors knew what he was going through, I say that because they knew how they were treating him every day.

Omar looked at that place like he was on the battlefield, fighting with those 8 people against him and he felt the only way he could have stopped his pain from all the racism and hate was to end his life and to end their life as well. He wanted to make sure that they didn't hurt anyone else. He made himself a human sacrifice to stop those eight people from ever hurting anyone else again. That is why he said, "I wish I could have gotten more."

When he said that, I knew he was talking about the other racist people because he only went after the eight people most racist towards him.

I believe him because he gave up his own life and I am his mother and when I listened to the 9-1-1 call, I can hear the pain and hurt in his voice. And this is a very sad situation.

Omar knew that he had to be the human sacrifice because he was no longer willing to fight racism and he was tired and he also knew that when he made that decision, there would be no one there to help him. He knew without a doubt that once he killed the people that was the most racist, he had to take his own life.

We must not be fooled because Omar Shariff Thornton is a victim of circumstances due to institutional racism at its worst. And he was determined to stop those people so much that he was willing to give up his own life.

May God have mercy on our souls. Institutional racism has to end.

No mother or no one else for that matter should ever have to experience racism, especially institutional racism, which in my opinion is "legal" racism. Which means that legalized racism exists in almost every aspect of our lives and is embedded in the fabric of America.

It cost my child his life and 8 other people's lives.

Omar and I at our last breakfast together. My other son, Edward was there as well.

I have a page called the (Omar Shariff Thornton) OST Memorial Foundation page which was founded in order to bring awareness about the effects of institutional racism in all of its forms and it does exist, that is why Omar Shariff Thornton is not alive today and also 8 other people.

How many more people will have to lose their lives before racism will come to an end?

And when I see so many people who do not want me to talk about Omar Shariff Thornton, that makes me understand how racist America really is.

They want to pretend as if Omar did not exist.

Well guess what? God made him and God knows that he was a victim because God said all men are equal.

And that is how I raised him. And when he realized that he would not be respected as an equal and got to understand racism, he just didn't want to take it anymore.

Racism is a disease for the person that is doing it and it is a disease for the person that is receiving it.

There are never any winners in this situation and I lost my baby. He was my child, he was my best friend and he was my everything and no mother is supposed to lose her baby.

I hope we can take what happened here and we all can come together as Americans and figure out how to stop workplace abuse. No one should ever have to suffer through what I have been through nor should Omar.

What he went through, enough is enough and it is time for all eyes to open.

I understand that the people at that company did not understand the damage that they were doing.

I know that they did not understand, I didn't understand either.

If I did, I would have saved my son's life and if the people at that company understood, they would have saved nine lives that day. But if someone was there that knew about prevention and understood institutional racism, that tragedy would not have happened. And it is unacceptable workplace abuse; that's what ended Omar Shariff Thornton's life.

So just imagine, and this is the part that I found out after he passed away from the people that work at the Hartford Distributors. A noose found dangling around a replica of President Barack Obama's neck. There was graffiti on the walls, calling him out of his name, "Slow Mar" and so many things were done to him. His name sprawled on the bathroom walls, "Die Nigger Omar!" which was immediately taken down with no retribution from the companies higher ups. But as you can see; their actions caused him to have post-traumatic stress disorder.

LILLIE HOLLIDAY
THE VOICE OF OMAR SHARIFF THORNTON

And it is important to understand what happened Omar. He was a strong, physically fit individual with a good solid mind. They took him in as a perfect individual with no prior history, no record of being arrested, he was the best of the best and he was young. Driving ever since he turned 21, doing deliveries from state to state for 14 years before he went to that company.

What they did, they tore his life apart. And even worse, the tore mine and even their own lives apart for the cause of continuing their traditions of, Racism.

It was like they were not looking for a driver, but they were looking for someone that they could do anything that they wanted to and they needed that person to be black.

See the thing is, the Hartford Distributors would be covering two things. They would be fulfilling their quota of employing a minority in the drivers' position and they would have someone that they didn't have to give any respect to. And I believe that this practice has been going on for a long time and according to the people that I talked to; people that worked there at one time or another, said that they were also treated in the same way that my son was treated.

They informed me that they were treated as if they were nobodies, so I figured Omar was just another attempt to have someone black working there.

Business as usual. And now it all comes together for me of why they would hire him and treat him the way they did. And it all becomes so plain and clear to me because they just needed a minority, someone black.

That is one reason why I believe that Omar suffered at that place, through institutional racism. They always put one black person as a driver and they have been doing this for years.

So I believe that they became very good at doing what they did and they knew exactly how to mistreat him when he got there.

But after all of those years of mistreatment of black workers. This time, as we say where I'm from, (they got the wrong one).

The higher ups within the Hartford Distributors could have never imagined the results of their employees' racist actions. They allowed their employees to demonstrate racist actions and attitudes with no repercussions. And I say this because of the fact that they had no fear of putting racist graffiti on the walls and writing nigger. They were comfortable with those types of things in that workplace. And it is evident for the fact that they just wiped it off of the walls and that was it.

I say this because to my knowledge for 30 years, the Hartford Distributors hired only one black driver at a time. So with that being said, I know they had no love for my son and like he said in his last words, they had no respect for him either.

And then it was reported that Omar was up for a raise making approximately $40,000 a year. And that sounded as if they were doing him a favor. As if he was being treated fairly but in all actuality, when Omar ran his trucking business, he grossed over $200,000 in a year. So it was definitely not a step up for him and it was not about the money at all.

But I also wonder why they did so many things to Omar and then tried to act like they didn't do anything wrong.

Just having him as one young black man working in a position with 63 white men and no peers of his own, that was wrong in itself.

And then act like nothing was wrong and like it was okay to disrespect him; to the degree that they wrote graffiti on the wall with the slogan, "Die nigger, Omar.", then they followed it up with having surveillance put on him when he started driving. The only black driver had surveillance. What kind of life is that for him as a young African American driver and why didn't they have surveillance on all of the drivers?

To me that looks like racism and that is exactly what Omar was referring to at the end of his life.

His last words to me was, "They treat me bad, and they treat all of the black people here bad."

So I know he was not in a good place, nor a good state of mind. Especially when he was driving to work that day listening to Eminem.

LILLIE HOLLIDAY
THE VOICE OF OMAR SHARIFF THORNTON

I listened to that song and I hurt just a little bit more. At one point in that song Eminem said "I'm not building my life over again." which is one of the same statements Omar said to me at the end. And he said "I'm not building my life over again."

It was so little that I understood at that point.

But at the end of the day, Omar was a strong black man and the system of institutional racism broke him down mentally and physically. But he never gave up, in his mind. He believed that he had picked up the tower for justice, for everyone and then he made himself a human sacrifice to it.

That is a very sad thing.

But the thing is, what happened to Omar, is still going on today.

And now people are still afraid to talk about it and racism still exists. Black people are still at a disadvantage, as long as the policies that are in place, still exist.

We are still training people to be our supervisors and not get the opportunity ourselves because of the color of our skin.

Omar understood all too well, just how his life was and he also understand how life was supposed to be. He also understood the color of his skin separated him and that he would never be the same as everyone else. He was saying that he was not an equal person and in his mind there was nothing he could do to ever change that, except what he did that fateful day.

That's why I say so many times, when they say he was stealing. That was irrelevant because the outcome would have remained the same. And there would have been nothing that I could have said to change his mind, he had already hurt enough.

The bottom line is that the beer that they said he gave away, is a petty amount. What is 24 cans of beer every 2 or 3 weeks? Especially when the company gives more than that away to their employees.

But if he did do what they said he did, it was just enough for Omar to let them know how he really felt about that company.

However, I am only human and I mourn for my child. And I was very upset for many years.

But the world needs to know and understand that ever since my son lost his life, there has not been a moment that I didn't think about those other eight people that lost their lives as well. And in my heart I know that something had to go wrong and Omar was willing to give up his own life.

I will always believe that under the circumstances, my son was so hurt and so mistreated that he was willing to give up everything.

I often wonder what Omar would be like right now, had he lived. What would he have achieved by now? Because he was such an achiever. Would he have ventured out into different careers and learn different things?

Omar was not afraid of studying and going to school and improving himself, that was one of his major things. His next goal while working at the Hartford Distributors was to go back to school to become an LPN (licensed practical nurse). He was always trying to improve himself and he was never happy sitting still.

That is why he suffered so much, because he wanted the American dream.

May God be with him and may he rest in peace. May this action help someone and reflect on changing America and its belief systems and give everyone equal opportunities.

Racism and all of its forms took away from Omar and also from me, as his mother.

I will never see him alive again, I will never talk to him again, I will never hug him again, I will never laugh with him again, I will never see his children, he will never be married, he will never get to go on vacations and enjoy the finer things in life, all due to racism and hate.

I looked into Omar's eyes and loved how he taught me the meaning of having a son. He taught me unlimited love as his mother. And nothing could ever take that away from me.

That's in my heart and every day I miss him.

LILLIE HOLLIDAY
THE VOICE OF OMAR SHARIFF THORNTON

White racism changed the direction of black people's lives, giving the people of color very little to no power at all.
Albert Einstein called racism a disease of white people in his little-known fight for civil rights.
Jane Elliott, in 1992 said racism is a mental illness.

Martin Luther King said "I came to this house, the time has come when silence is a betrayal." The truth of those words came without a doubt and I wish to go on now and say something that is even more disturbing. You have to put a different face on what racism looks like before America can begin to heal.

We all have to recognize what the problems are and how institutional racism affects every aspect of our lives. We fight and deal with racism from the cradle to the grave and it is sad but at the end of his life he learned how much racism and hate is among his own people as well.

It kind of reminds me of the times when he was very young and around his sister. He would always say to her, "You give love a bad name." at any given moment, Omar had so many different challenges in his life. And in my opinion, challenges that should have never existed.

But in order to begin to heal, we have to bring awareness to the existence of institutional racism. And that is truly the only way we can end situations like the one that Omar faced when he was alive.

I believe not everyone but some people, say racist things because they are so used to the old way of thinking, which was accepted by the governing society. Some people may not even realize how much pain and hurt it brings to another person.

But it has to come out in the open and it has to Stop!

The perpetrators need to get rid of old habits that cause pain, especially when it is racially motivated. When it comes to my son, Omar Shariff Thornton, I believe that the people that he worked with demonstrated those old habits. But I have a feeling that within their hearts, they may not have had racist hearts, just bad habits. And when you compound those old bad habits with someone that was already affected by racism, what happened at the Hartford Distributors can happen. Because Omar was not willing to accept it anymore.

But it seems like almost every other week, there is someone in a high position getting caught saying something or doing something that would be considered racist behavior. And then when it is exposed to the world, everyone wants to sweep it under the rug and not get to the healing part of the situation.

But the point that I'm trying to make is that when racism is brought out in the open, you get a chance to heal but when it's done in private no one sees it and there is no lesson to be learned and no healing to be done.

But institutional racism, at its worst, is a disease that can become an uncontrollable disease. A disease that would cause a person that administers it to lose themselves and the person receiving it to lose themselves as well.

And it is a sad situation and it has to come to an end.

My condolences go out to all the families that are involved, we are all hurting and may God be with us and help us learn from this situation. Help all of us to heal and make America a better place. With America standing together as one, we will be the strongest country in the world forever.

And the story does not end here...

Author's note:

Let me briefly talk about Omar's relationship with his girlfriend's family. Omar spent a great deal of time with her brother, who was so broken up after Omar's death that he was stressed out and went through so many different emotions. They were so close and had made a connection. And he was also close to her mother even though she did not like him in the beginning and she treated him badly. He was never disrespectful despite all of that.

But when she saw that he was such a good person and how well he treated her daughter and her son, she had a change of heart.

She has since passed away and may she rest in peace. My condolences go out to her son.

LILLIE HOLLIDAY
THE VOICE OF OMAR SHARIFF THORNTON

Lillie Holliday's thoughts...

We have more people in prison than any other country, mainly blacks and Latinos. We as black people suffer more in America than any other race and it seems like we can never pay off our debt for being brought to America as slaves.

We provided free labor for 400 years and it is still not enough. We are the last to get hired, we don't have the best schools and we don't have the best of anything in America.

Collectively, we don't own anything that has real value and in America, we as black people face the hardest times. Even to the point where we have our young men dying on the streets by the hands of the police. The main ones that are supposed to protect us.

We as black people feel the threat from everywhere, even when we try our hardest, it is still not easy to escape.

The playing field has to level itself so that we as a people can survive.

I taught Omar to have his own business and that was not enough to escape from the throngs of prejudice and racism. He was still taken advantage of.

I just didn't really realize how hard it would be for him to try to do the right thing. And as a young black man it was almost like the more he tried the more the obstacles would stand in his way.

For a young black man in Omar's case and having no prior records, he was like a target for the police department. It seemed as though, all they wanted to do was find a way to stop him and give him some kind of a criminal record.

So not only was he up against prejudice, racism and institutional racism, he was up against the forces of it.

But he was still trying to survive as an honest young man and just wanted to achieve the American dream. But he had no idea how hard the battle would be because I always told him that he was equal to everyone. And he believed in that philosophy of life. But now I know that it just made things even harder for him. And there's so many people that has had the same experience that Omar had.

But whenever I mention Omar's name to someone, they always tell me how they understand exactly what he was going through. And they would go on to tell me how they had been through what he had been through, so many times. And they would express how they wanted to do exactly what he did. And one of them went on to tell me how their health got affected, telling me stories of how they got sick from the anxiety and the pressure of working in a toxic environment.

I've even had some people tell me that they ended up in a mental institution because of workplace abuse. And some would tell me how they had almost lost their minds. Some are still dealing with mental conditions due to the workplace environment.

The things that happened to them and the stories that were told sounded just unbelievable. But everyone cannot just walk away from their jobs.

Some people just stay there until their health becomes completely ruined and where they can no longer help themselves.

And in America today, it is just sad when I turn the television on just to see them shooting down young black men. They are killing them or beating a black woman in the streets or beating up our children in the schools.

Blacks are paying the most money in the criminal system, blacks get the most time in jail for their crimes. Blacks are the last to get hired and the first to get fired. The system is geared against black people in America and my son learned that the hard way.

The racist policies that were put in place so many years before now is the reason why so many of our black kids are dying today in the streets of the inner cities.

Institutional Racism is on the same category as a Hate Crime. And Hate Crime Laws were just signed in 2009 by President Barack Obama.

I just can't believe that after all those years of slavery, the United States took so long to sign a bill like that.

How many more black people will have to lose their lives or their minds before Congress will recognize a need for a law to stop Institutional Racism?

I want to see the day when I don't have to tell my grandchildren how to prepare themselves to not get killed by the police and the day that they don't have to face institutional racism. And I want to see the day when all people can become equal. Racism is not just about black and white.

And now I really understand all of the obstacles that was in front of him and how he just wasn't willing to keep on dealing with it.

So in his mind, he thought that he could shine a light on racism. He also knew that he was bringing the end to some of the most racist people that he had ever met in his lifetime.

But please keep in mind and remember that it is not important to focus on whether or not racism exists at that place, it is only important to learn that Omar believed that it existed and that is what ultimately pushed him over the edge.

Racism has so many different forms, that is why I always say that institutional racism and racism has to come to an end in all of its forms.

Omar Shariff Thornton

Long before that dreadful day in Manchester, Ct, Omar Shariff Thornton's life really ended.

There were signs that he was preparing for it to end, that was not detected at the time.

He closed down his apartment and he had picked out some of his clothes to give to his brother.

He got his brother to go with him to sell all of his guns except for the ones that he used in the shootings.

I still didn't see what he was doing at the time.

I remember that he used up all of his credit cards, but I should have known something was wrong because he loved his guns and he took a lot of time to build his credit up.

Omar did a good job hiding his secret from me. But at the end of his life, he wanted to take something from them because he had so much taken from him.

And at the end of his life, he had no respect for those people or that job any longer.

But I think he just wanted to send a strong message that they were going to feel what he felt for so many years.

He had so much happen to him, from some of the jobs that had taken advantage of him. And sadly, as a result, he felt cornered and he had no way out.

In his heart and in his mind, Omar believed that the way he went out of this life was the only way out.

No, he never threw down the towel, he actually picked up the towel for justice and to fight against institutional racism.

The saddest part about this, is that every time I think about it; it just kind of takes my breath away.

LILLIE HOLLIDAY
THE VOICE OF OMAR SHARIFF THORNTON

The bullet that he used to kill himself.

I gave him that bullet...

All of the bullets that we used for our guns were all hollow.

Omar came to me 6 weeks before his life ended and asked me to give him a bullet.

Our bullets were all hollow but I had the only bullet that was not hollow.

I had those bullets for years, so when he asked me for one, I didn't give it a second thought at all but even then, he was at that point where he was going to end his life.

Now you might be wondering at the significance of him asking for a regular bullet as opposed to a hollow one.

Well you see, Omar was still thinking about how to protect me even after his death because he just knew that I would have seen the condition that his body would have been in. If he would have used those hollow bullets, he would not have been recognizable. The hollow bullets would have destroyed his body and he still did not want me to see that. So he used the bullet that I gave to him because it would not tear his body up.

But ironically, I did not want to remember Omar not alive.

So I tell you that Omar never missed a beat. He thought about all of the things that were important.

His mind was made up and that is all that mattered to him.

Omar was willing to give up his life at 34 year's old.

He said to me that he had nowhere else to go and that he was cornered. The system was against him, the company that he work for and the people that work there was also against him.

Not everyone but just the eight people that he went after and ended their lives.

And that is very sad because there are no winners in this situation.

Omar is also a victim of circumstances, just to imagine someone at the age of 34 years old and willing to give up their life.

He was only trying to make America a better place for everyone. And he believed in his mind that what he did would help stop racism. And that he would pave the path for others not to suffer what he suffered. And it was that path that wounded him mentally, until he could not save himself.

But now in modern day society, slavery is apparent through treatment, mentally and physically. And blacks are still being abused and mistreated in so many different ways and it is still being covered up.

The things that happened to Omar and that pushed him over the edge were the same types of things that people go through and have been for hundreds of years.

The hiring practices,
Bullying,
Talking down to,
Verbal abuse,
Emotional abuse,
Name calling,
Targeting,
Unfair treatment,
Being ignored,
Noose around the black presidents neck,
Abusive conduct,
Harassing,
Black jokes, Humiliating
Graffiti on the walls depicting negativity towards people of color!
Racially insensitive pictures, deceiving, lies and cover-ups.

I learned that these things are what happened to him at the Hartford Distributors after he had passed away. And I was told by the people that worked for that company.

They came on television and talked about the way they treated him to the news reporters and that's how I found out about what he was going through. And that is very sad but something that a lot of black people go through today.

LILLIE HOLLIDAY
THE VOICE OF OMAR SHARIFF THORNTON

They just don't talk about it because they are afraid of losing their jobs, but they suffer from it through their health. Their having heart attacks, strokes, and all different sicknesses from that kind of treatment.

They get stressed out and it leads to so many other different things and it is still the type of suffering that goes on in the workplace today. And it is very well covered up because people don't want to talk about it. They suffer in private until their bodies just can't take it anymore and then they break down from one or another type of sickness.

The younger generation, they will be dealing with this situation differently, so we need to be aware of what is going on. They will not tolerate it the same way the older generation has. And I don't want anyone going through what I have gone through in these last few years. And I did everything in my power not to lose my mind and thank God I am still here.

We have children that are mixed with every nationality that you could think of. And there is a need for respect for the human race and God made all of us equal.

Omar's Final Words

On 8/3/2010, these are the final words that Omar said to me.

In that last 7 minutes he called me,

Omar- *"Good morning mom, turn the TV off. I have to tell you something that is real serious. I killed the 5 most racist people and I'm going to end my own life and I want you to know that these people have treated me bad. They're racist they have no respect for me and they have been hurting black people for a long time and what I do realize is that there will not be no place for black people in America unless I make this sacrifice to try and change things. I want you to realize there is things in the house that I want you to be able to find, so I'm going to tell you where I put everything, so that you will find them. Don't be upset mom, this is the only decision for me to make. I've tried everything in this life and it just doesn't get better. I love you mom and I love my family. This decision would change things for all of us in this lifetime."*

And while he was talking, I can hear the pain, the hurt and the sadness in his voice. I know he just wished it was a different way out But he continued on,

Omar- *"Mom, I tried everything, but this world has no place for me as a black man and everything has failed me here. Racism and hate has to stop mom. I did everything I could but (still) the demons of hate and racism is still after me. Mom please don't worry about me, I'm doing exactly what I have to do and everything is going to be ok. I love you but I got to go now."*

After that conversation with my baby, I don't even want to talk about me right now. I don't even want to talk about what I'm feeling because I can't.

There is no way to explain my hurt right now and the only thing that I could say to Omar was,

Me- "Omar! I love you. I love you more than life itself."

Omar- "I love you."

And then all of a sudden I heard the phone click and go dead.

That was the end. The last conversation with my baby, Omar Shariff Thornton. He will forever be missed and loved always.

"Injustice Anywhere is A Threat to Justice Everywhere." Dr. Martin Luther King, Jr.

Omar at one of his last cook out's. He enjoyed spending time with his family and friends. He will be missed.

Omar and I, in loving memory of happier times in our lives. In this picture, I surround my baby with love.

Edward and Omar having good times.

LILLIE HOLLIDAY
THE VOICE OF OMAR SHARIFF THORNTON

Edward and his brother Omar as young boys.

Thoughts from Omar's Brother...

My brother was my best friend and my right hand man.

I miss him so much. You always think you are supposed to go before your younger brother but you can't predict the future and the impact certain things will have on a person's life.

I remember when my brother first started working for Hartford Distributers, he was excited but after a while he would tell me that they were racist and treated him bad. Me, being a big brother and understanding what he was going through, I told him to brush it off and just do his job because it was a good job with good benefits, so he agreed. But I did not know what he was really going through because he was the type of person not to reveal his true feelings.

My brother was not a violent man, it took a lot to get him upset but he went through a lot in his short time on this planet.

He always wanted to be an entrepreneur but things always got in his way. He never stopped trying though. Omar was a good man with a big heart, I like to think he learned from my mistakes and vowed to make his life different from the way mine was. We were the total opposite.

I know I made bad choices in life but I like to think that my mistakes showed him how to do the right thing. To be strong.

It's just sad that he did everything right and still had to go through what he went through. Since my brother passed, I have really tried to live the life that he wanted me to live. He is my hero and I will forever be grateful for what he stood for.

So when my uncle and I were on our way to the police station after talking to my mom, who had announced that something had happened with my brother. My uncle proceeded to chant, "He's dead, he's dead!" He said it in such a negative manner that it tore me apart and made me so upset that I wanted to punch my own uncle for being that insensitive. That was a dark day for me.

But his death was a wakeup call for me and got me on my feet. I love my brother so much that I wanted to show him even though he is not here that I would be the person he always wanted me to be.

Racism plays a part in our lives all around the world and it's sad my little brother had to be a victim to it.

I love you Omar and I will forever miss you. God bless.

Your memory will always remain in my heart.

Edward...

LILLIE HOLLIDAY
THE VOICE OF OMAR SHARIFF THORNTON

Omar Shariff Thornton will never, ever be forgotten!

His Voice will live on Forever!

Thank you for your support

Thank you for your support!

Lillie Holliday